# Watching Lacandon Maya Lives

# Watching Lacandon Maya Lives

**R. Jon McGee**

*Southwest Texas State University*

**Allyn and Bacon**

Boston ■ London ■ Toronto ■ Sydney ■ Tokyo ■ Singapore

**Series Editor:** *Jennifer Jacobson*
**Editor-in-Chief, Social Sciences:** *Karen Hanson*
**Series Editorial Assistant:** *Tom Jefferies*
**Senior Marketing Manager:** *Judeth Hall*
**Production Administrator:** *Beth Houston*
**Editorial-Production Service:** *Omegatype Typography, Inc.*
**Composition and Prepress Buyer:** *Linda Cox*
**Manufacturing Manager:** *Joanne Sweeney*
**Cover Administrator:** *Kristina Mose-Libon*
**Cover Designer:** *Joel Gendron*
**Electronic Composition:** *Omegatype Typography, Inc.*

**Library of Congress Cataloging-in-Publication Data**

McGee, R. Jon
    Watching Lacandon Maya lives / R. Jon McGee.
        p.   cm.
    Includes bibliographical references and index.
    ISBN 0-205-33218-8 (alk. paper)
        1. Lacandon Indians.   I. Title.

F1221.L2 M425 2002
972'.004974152–dc21

                                        2001024968

Printed in the United States of America

*To my wife Stacie and our children Jake and Hannah.*
*Thank you for forgiving my absences and*
*making it worth coming home.*

# CONTENTS

# INTRODUCTION

In the spring of 1980 I was a single, twenty-four-year-old graduate student at Rice University in Houston, Texas. I was studying anthropology, and was busy with my classes and a part-time job in the University Library, but I had a problem. I had been studying a discipline that said real anthropologists did fieldwork, preferably in an exotic setting. I had no fieldwork project. I had studied religion and religious symbolism, and in college had developed an interest in ethnographic filmmaking, but where could all this book knowledge be put into practice? I didn't have a clue.

One afternoon I walked in on a conversation between my filmmaking professor Brian Hubermann and an anthropologist named Mike Rees. I gathered from the conversation that Mike Rees had conducted his fieldwork a decade previously with a people called the Lacandon, that they were Maya, and lived in a rain forest somewhere in Mexico. Rees and Hubermann were planning a return trip to make an ethnographic film and record the changes in Lacandon society during the last ten years. I heard "Maya" and "jungle" and started having visions of tropical adventures. Although I had never been to Mexico, didn't speak a word of Spanish, and hardly knew Maya from Aztec, Zapotec, or Olmec, I volunteered to be a gopher for the project if I could accompany them on the trip.

I had no idea what I was volunteering for. If I had thought about some of the dangers such as malaria, hepatitis, and poisonous snakes I might have had second thoughts. If I could have foreseen some of the trials I would endure in Chiapas, such as lying in a hammock too weak to move from food poisoning with my tongue turning black, or walking the streets of Palenque one night, semidelirious with a fever so high I thought it was the following morning, or bent over on hands and knees by the side of a jungle road vomiting while a busload of Maya Indians watched impassively from the windows, I might have had second thoughts. But I thought little about anything other than the excitement of leaving for Mexico. Mike and I left in May of 1980, returned to Houston in August, and I was hooked on Chiapas. I have been back to Mexico at least once a year ever since.

I am writing now in the spring of 2001, twenty-one years since that first trip. Much of what I found in those jungle communities twenty years ago no longer exists. But then the young man who went there is gone too. A lot has happened in twenty years. My original guide, Mike Rees, left anthropology to practice law in a small town in southeast Texas. The twenty-four-year-old grad student became an anthropology professor taking students on their first trips to Mexico. The sense of adventure that was so much a part of that first trip into the Lacandon Jungle wore off long ago. However, the craving for adventure has been replaced by a love and respect for the people who taught me their language, and shared their homes, food, and knowledge. Where I was once seeking adventure, returning to Chiapas now I am excited by the prospect of greeting old friends, hearing family news, holding new babies, and passing pictures of my wife and children around a circle of eager hands.

Writing a book is an arduous process and much of what has driven me to sit down and write is the respect and affection that I feel for the Lacandon. The Lacandon Maya have been caricatured, romanticized, misrepresented, and stereotyped by virtually everyone who has had casual contact with them or written about them in the popular press. Typically, they are presented as exotic jungle people who practice ancient Maya rituals and commune with the forest, but who are unsophisticated in the ways of the civilized world. However, the currents of national economic forces, in particular the boom and bust of the Mexican oil economy, tourism, and political rebellion are the wider stage on which the last few generations of Lacandon have lived out their lives. The Lacandon economy has transformed from one largely based on swidden horticulture to a mixed economy in which tourism plays an important role. Electricity, television, and satellite programming arrived in the Lacandon communities in the early 1990s, about the same time that they abandoned their non-Christian religious practices.

The Lacandon people shared their lives with me and gave me the information that helped me make my career as an anthropologist. To a large degree who and what I am is due to their kindness and generosity. It is time now to start giving back. I feel I owe my Lacandon friends a book that attempts to describe their lives and my experience with them as accurately as possible. In this book I follow the lives of individuals in one large extended Lacandon family over three generations as a way to make sense of the social and cultural transitions through which the Lacandon have passed in the last twenty years. Additionally, I wrote this book to raise money for the Lacandon Medical Fund administered by the Asociación Cultural Na Bolom in San Cristobal, Chiapas. Na Bolom is a small nonprofit organization founded by Franz and Trudi Blom as a museum, library, and center for the study of the Maya. The Asociación oversees a variety of projects that promote the welfare of the Lacandon, one of which is the Lacandon Medical Fund. The Lacandon communities today have small clinics that provide basic medical care. However, for significant medical problems they have to go to San Cristobal. Na Bolom provides them a place to stay and pays for needed medical services. It is no surprise that demand for medical care sometimes overwhelms Na Bolom's resources. This book is my way of thanking the Lacandon for their kindness over the years and providing a gift that will benefit them all.

## Acknowledgments

The information presented in this book was made possible by the support of several institutions. I wish to acknowledge the support of the Wenner Gren Foundation for Anthropological Research, the American Council of Learned Societies, the National Geographic Society, and the Office of Research and Sponsored Programs at Southwest Texas State University. I also owe a great debt to my colleagues Rich Warms, Ana Juarez, and Don Kurtz. Rich and Don lent me their considerable organizational and editorial expertise during the preparation of this manuscript. Ana first got me thinking about the significance of gender to my work and what exactly was meant by *traditional* Lacandon. My friend and fact checker, Dan Renshaw, also deserves a note of thanks. Dan's marriage to a Lacandon woman gives him a unique perspective on Lacandon life, and his observations and comments have given me many valuable insights I might otherwise have missed. I also need to thank my colleague Britt Bousman for his map-making expertise and the Asociación Cultural Na Bolom for permission to use one of Gertrude Duby-Blom's photographs. Finally I would like to thank my student and friend Ryan Kashanipour for his work in Lacanha, his contribution to Chapter 6, and his tireless pursuit of obscure publications about the Lacandon.

I would like to think that the last twenty years of work has given me some insights that are worth sharing into how anthropological fieldwork is practiced and reported. In particular, I have seen firsthand the ways in which events in my life have affected the information that I had access to, the questions I asked, and the way I reported what I found. I now examine very carefully what I think I know and how I have come to know it. In essence, I can no longer write much about the Lacandon without also thinking about how events in my own life steered me toward certain observations and conclusions. To talk about the Lacandon is also to talk about my relationships with them. I have become very sensitive to those who claim to speak for the Lacandon or know what is best for them, particularly when those self-appointed spokespersons do not speak Maya, have spent limited time in the different Lacandon communities, and stand to profit from what they say.

The heart of this book is an analysis of the material and economic changes that have occurred in the community of Nahá over the last twenty years and the different adaptations that families within one large extended kin group have made to the changing world around them. However, the things I noticed, the people I talked to, and the questions I asked them are in large part a reflection of what was going on in my life during those times. So that readers have a better idea of how I came to know what I have written about the Lacandon and how I reached the conclusions I make, I have included a great deal about my experiences with them. It is a materialist analysis written in a reflexive style that I hope will be accessible to anyone who picks up the book. At the end of the book you will find an extensive glossary of Spanish and Maya terms that are used in the text. Additionally, the appendix is a kinship chart of the family featured in Chapters 3 and 4. In Chapter 4, individuals are numbered, for example, Kayum #14, to indicate their position on this kin chart. If you wish to share your own thoughts with me I can be reached at the Department of Anthropology, Southwest Texas State University in San Marcos, Texas, or e-mailed at rm08@swt.edu.

Jon McGee

# 1 Lacandon: The Last Lords of the Rain Forest?

## Romantic Images

For 150 years, writers have painted a romanticized portrait of the Lacandon Maya as either a simple, pristine people living in isolated splendor in the rain forest or as the last vestige of Classic Period Maya society. Nineteenth-century explorers in the Lacandon Jungle, interested in the origins of ancient Maya civilization, imagined the Lacandon were the direct descendants of the ancient Maya of Palenque, Yaxchilan, and Bonampak. They assumed this in part because the Lacandon were non-Christian and lived in close proximity to these sites. This image of the Lacandon was initially spread by the writings of nineteenth-century travelers to Mexico. In particular, works such as John L. Stephens's *Incidents of Travel in Central America, Chiapas, and Yucatan,* Desiré Charnay's *Ancient Cities in the New World,* and Alfred Maudsley's *Biologia Centrali-Americana* fostered a romantic fascination with the rise and fall of ancient Maya civilization and typically linked the Lacandon to the mysterious ruins illustrated in their accounts. An example that is typical of writing of this period is Fredrick Boyle's comment in the *Transactions of the Ethnological Society of London:*

> Certainly the Lacandones and their country, so mysterious and romantic, offer one of the most interesting subjects of exploration left in the world. Whether or no we believe in the Itzimaya, the great city of golden mystery, we must at least feel a thrill of excitement in reflecting that a territory exists in which such a romance is possible. (1867:210)

Consequently, adventure on their minds and romance in their hearts, the first Lacandon ethnographers went into Lacandon settlements looking for traces of that long-lost civilization. For instance, Karl Sapper, who visited two Lacandon communities in the 1890s, wrote:

> While it is true that there are many peoples in a natural state on the earth today already near extinction, and probably significant and interesting data might be obtained from them all, yet it must still be of especial importance to listen to the beliefs of the Lacandons and to investigate their customs, for thereby, despite the, of course, already much altered and varied form, there must still fall many a revealing light on the mysterious mythology and remarkable customs of the ancient civilized nation of the Maya. (1897:264)

The search for traces of the ancient Maya among the Lacandon continued into the twentieth century. In 1901, Harvard anthropologist Alfred M. Tozzer who was searching for survivals from the ancient Maya past spent several weeks living with a Lacandon family. Tozzer specifically looked for knowledge of hieroglyphic writing among the Lacandon. He even brought a copy of an ancient Maya codex with him to show to his hosts. However, like those before him, Tozzer was frustrated in this aspect of his quest. Tozzer noted numerous parallels between Lacandon and ancient Maya religions and believed that there had been little European influence on the Lacandon. Thus he concluded that the religious practices he observed were survivals of ancient Maya rituals (1907:284).

Forty years later, David Amram visited a Lacandon camp occupied by a man named Chan K'in, whose father, Jose Bol Garcia, had been Tozzer's primary informant near Lake Pethá. Amram too believed the Lacandon to be a cultural holdover from the ancient Maya. In his 1941 article "The Lacandon, Last of the Maya," he wrote:

> The Classic Maya were destroyed, but a few primitive groups allied to them survived, only because they lived in wild, untractable regions, far removed from the trails of the marauding Spaniard. Of these few groups, the most interesting is that known as the Lacandon. (15)

Howard Cline said much the same thing three years later. Cline wrote, "Isolated geographically, the relatively slight contacts that Lacandones have had with westernized cultures have permitted apparent survival of numerous old Mayan traits and practices" (1944:107).

Tozzer, Amram, and Cline wrote long enough ago that the constellation of romanticized nineteenth-century themes they perpetuated might have died were it not for the 1982 publication of the book *The Last Lords of Palenque* by Robert Bruce and Victor Perera. Bruce and Perera claimed not only that the Lacandon were the only cultural heirs of ancient Maya civilization, but also that the Lacandon were direct descendants of the Maya of Palenque. They further asserted that an elder in the community named Chan K$^?$in Viejo was "not only Lord of Palenque, but the last of the *halach winik* (great lords) of the Olmec-Maya tradition" (1982:13). *The Last Lords* gave new life to the nineteenth-century romanticism with which people approached the Lacandon. Even now, almost two decades after its publication, I still encounter travelers to Nahá looking for the society of jungle ecologists/philosophers described in this book.

The mythology of the Lacandon, perpetuated until very recently by most of the people who have written about them, revolves around three themes:

1. The Lacandon are the descendants of the builders of the great Maya sites such as Palenque and Yaxchilan.
2. Looking at Lacandon culture today is a window into ancient Maya life.
3. The Lacandon have preserved the ancient culture because they were hidden deep in the forest and isolated from the rest of the world.

In this chapter, I would like to review what is known about the origins of the people who today are called the Lacandon and examine what we know of the lives of those people who long ago inhabited the forests of eastern Chiapas and western Guatemala. I will also address the myths that have interfered with an accurate perception of Lacandon society for almost two hundred years.

First, after decades of linguistic and historical study and advances in decipherment of Maya writing, it is widely accepted that the original inhabitants of lowland Chiapas sites such as Palenque and Yaxchilan were speakers of Chol Maya, not the dialect of Yucatec Maya spoken by the modern Lacandon, and that the Last Lords of Palenque scenario is a nineteenth-century romantic fantasy. There is no longer a large population of Chol speakers in the area today because they were forcibly removed or killed off by the Spaniards in the sixteenth and seventeenth centuries.

Contributing to the misunderstanding of the Lacandon and their origins has been the lack of precision with which the Spaniards employed the term *Lacandon*. During the sixteenth and seventeenth centuries, the Spaniards indiscriminately used the term *Lacandon* to refer to all unpacified and non-Christian people in what is today southeastern Chiapas and northwestern Guatemala, in particular the area bounded by the Usumacinta, Pasión, and Jatate River drainages (see Map 1.1). This is important because until recently most of those writing about the Lacandon did not make a thorough distinction between the sixteenth-century Chol-speaking Lacandon population and the Yucatec-speaking Lacandon who appeared in the historical record in the second half of the eighteenth and early nineteenth centuries.

## Sixteenth and Seventeenth Centuries: Chol-Lacandon

Chol-speaking Lacandon inhabited the Chiapas lowlands until the early 1700s. However, those who chronicled events on the seventeenth-century Spanish frontier tell us that huge numbers of Chol were killed through warfare, disease, and forced labor (Soto-Mayor 1983; Ximinez 1929–1931). Nations (1979:43) estimates that 90 percent of the Chol population was eliminated or removed from the western lowlands by 1712.

Initial Spanish contact with the Chol-Lacandon was made in 1530 when members of the Davila expedition accidentally stumbled on Lake Lacandon (renamed Lake Miramar in 1928) and briefly occupied the Chol community they found on an island in the lake. However, finding no riches they soon moved on. Future contacts between Spaniard and Chol were less benign. In 1559, Ramirez de Quiñones led an *entrada* (armed expedition) back to Lake Miramar and sacked the settlements on the lake.

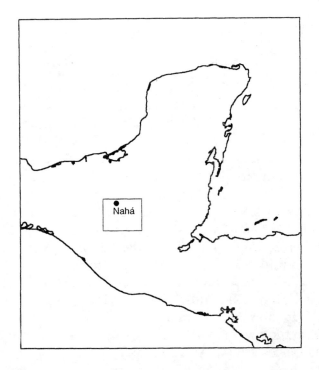

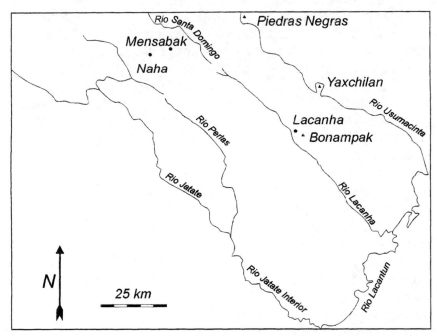

**MAP 1.1   The Lacandon Jungle.**

In 1586, Juan de Morales de Villavicencio returned to Lake Lacandon and destroyed the island fortress of Lacantun which had been reoccupied by Chol-Lacandon in the twenty-five years since the Quiñones expedition. Those inhabitants who did not escape into the forest were killed or sold into slavery.

The conquistadors were savage in their treatment of the native peoples of the Americas, who they viewed as little more than beasts of burden to be worked to death and replaced. Those Chol-Lacandon who survived the predation of the first wave of Spaniards looking for gold and military fame then had to endure the Catholic priests and friars who were intent on saving their souls. Hundreds of people who had not died in the initial battles and epidemics of smallpox and measles were resettled into frontier settlements, such as Comitan, Palenque, and Ocosingo. Chol-Lacandon populations were removed from the Chiapas and Guatemala lowlands in the *reducciones* of Pochutla in 1564 and Lake Lacandon in 1586. Most of those who refused resettlement were killed in later Spanish raids.

During the seventeenth century, there was a continuation of previous policies with alternating military and missionary expeditions into the Lacandon Jungle to subdue and resettle Chol communities. The last great effort to pacify the Chol-Lacandon was conducted in 1695. A three-pronged advance into Lacandon territory was planned by the president of the *Audiencia* of Gualtemala, Jacinto de Barrios Leal. The *entrada* led by Barrios Leal left Ocosingo on February 29, 1695. On April 6, 1695, after a long and difficult journey, they came to the Lacandon town of Sac Balam. Sac Balam was described as a town of "a hundred good private houses" (Tozzer 1984:3), with a population of four hundred to five hundred. The town was peacefully occupied by the Spaniards on April 19 and renamed Nuestra Señora de los Dolores de Lacandon. The mission to convert the Chol-Lacandon in Dolores was directed by Father Antonio Margil, who briefly described events around the mission in letters to his superiors dated between May and August 1695 (Leutenegger and Habig 1976). In 1696, the last two Chol-Lacandon towns were contacted by missionaries from Dolores and resettled into a new mission community called San Ramon. By 1696, the conquest of the Chol-Lacandon was complete, with the originally estimated population of 4,000 to 7,000 Chol-Lacandon reduced to around 1,000 (Nations 1979:71).

# Eighteenth Century: Yucatec-Lacandon

The conquest of the Chiapas jungle yielded little of value to the Spaniards. Eighteenth-century Spaniards generally considered the tropical lowland forests to be uninhabitable. Because there were no precious metals or large pools of human labor to exploit for agriculture, the conquistadors were generally unwilling to settle or build haciendas in the jungle, preferring instead to colonize more temperate areas outside the forest. Lacking significant support, jungle communities like Dolores and San Ramon were abandoned by 1712. Consequently, the main result of a century of Spanish effort was the depopulation of the eastern Chiapas–western Guatemala forests and the creation of what Palka (1998:461) calls a "free zone" for Maya escaping Spanish rule.

After the removal of the Chol-Lacandon population, groups of Yucatec-speaking Lacandon, primarily from the Peten area of western Guatemala, began to trickle into the area and establish communities in the territory formerly inhabited by Chol speakers. Throughout the eighteenth century, these refugees moved westward through the Peten and into Chiapas and it is among these immigrants that we find the ancestors of the modern Lacandon.

The history of events in the eastern Chiapas jungle during the seventeenth and early eighteenth century is complex and confused by scarce historical data. The jungle was a refuge for many different Maya groups who lived in dispersed settlements, avoided areas controlled by the Spaniards, and were generally left alone. It is impossible to conclusively trace the movements of the modern Lacandons' ancestors during this period, though numerous scholars have tried (see Scholes and Roys 1968; Thompson 1970; Hellmuth 1972; De Vos 1980). However, there are numerous historical records from the 1780s and 1790s that describe families we can confidently link to the modern Lacandon.

First contact between Spaniards and people who were certainly ancestors of the modern Lacandon occurred in 1786 when Father Manuel Calderón, the parish priest of Palenque, encountered Yucatec-Lacandon several leagues (a league is about 3 miles) southeast of Palenque. Father Calderón initiated several visits with these families and over the next few years they began to visit him in Palenque, taking meals with the priest and trading cacao and other forest products for tools, salt, and medicines. During the 1790s, contact between Lacandon and the townspeople of Palenque became regular enough that a few Lacandon men married women from Palenque and their children were baptized (Boremanse 1998:5).

It took Father Calderón several years to acquire funds to establish a mission for the Lacandon, but in June and July of 1793 he established the hamlet of San José de Gracia Real at a site chosen by the Lacandon because it was near their cornfields (DeVos 1980:225). San José was about eight leagues southeast of Palenque, and strategically located for trade. The Lacandon there apparently acted as middlemen for trade between the people of Palenque and the Lacandon groups farther south in the forest. Lacandon from the southern forest brought honey, wax, cacao, corn, cotton, and tobacco to trade with their comrades in San José for salt, cloth, beads, and iron tools. In turn, the people of San José sold forest products to the people of Palenque and other Christianized Indians.

Father Calderón established the community of San José in June 1793, and by the time he returned to Palenque on July 20, 43 people had established residence in San José and 103 more had promised to settle there (DeVos 1980:225). The Lacandon at San José received a continual supply of gifts (e.g., cotton cloth, ribbons, steel axes, and machetes) from Father Calderón as a part of his program to convert them to Christianity. However, despite his best efforts, the people of San José learned little of Christianity. Despite Father Calderón's repeated requests to his superiors the community never had a full-time priest or friar to minister to them and the local religious authorities did not speak Yucatec Lacandon. After Father Calderón's death in 1797, the commerce between San José and Palenque continued, especially trade in tobacco, but the Lacandon gradually began to drift away from the settlement. By 1800, there were only thirty or so people. Visitors to San José wrote that few children were being baptized and the adults continued to worship their idols according to their old customs in a temple hidden at the edge of the community, while at the same time attending Catholic services. By 1807, the site was completely abandoned (DeVos 1980:226–227).

From the reports written by Calderón and government officials who visited San José it is clear that at least some the community's inhabitants were ancestors of the contemporary Lacandon. The appearance of the two groups was virtually identical. Like the modern Lacandon the men of San José let their hair grow long and wore white knee-length tunics. Women wore the same tunic over a skirt and bead necklaces around their necks. Like the modern population, they preferred to live in dispersed settlements near their *milpas*. Their homes were thatched huts with no walls, and they slept in hammocks.

Subsistence and marriage practices were also similar. Like the modern Lacandon, they cultivated a wide variety of crops including corn, beans, tobacco, annatto, cotton, manioc, sweet potatoes, avocado, and orange and lemon trees, and they were avid hunters and fishers. Like Lacandon in the twentieth century, the Lacandon of San José practiced first-cousin marriage and were polygynous (Nations 1979:92).

Descriptions of the religious activity at San José are limited, but the non-Christian rites practiced there sound much like those of the Lacandon in the twentieth century. San José Lacandon prayed to incense burners that they kept sheltered in a ceremonial hut at the edge of the community in the same way that non-Christian Lacandon today maintain a *yatoch k'uh*, or god house, on the periphery of their household clusters.

Most importantly, from Spanish censuses we know that people with four of the twelve *onen* names carried by contemporary Lacandon lived in San José (DeVos 1980:227). The *onen* is a patrilineally inherited animal name that functions something like a surname. So in Nahá today a man named K'in who belonged to the *ma'ax* (spider monkey) *onen* would probably give his name as K'in Ma'ax, and all of his children would be members of the *ma'ax onen*. Additionally, by 1900 many men and women of the *ma'ax onen* had also adopted the Spanish surname García. Table 1.1 lists the contemporary Lacandon *onens* and those named in the seventeenth century census at San José. One can see that members of the Koho', Nahwahto', Haawo', and Puko' *onens* were all present in San José.

It is clear that at least some of the families of San José were ancestors of some contemporary Lacandon. However, when San

**TABLE 1.1**  Lacandon *Onen*

| Ceremonial Name | Common Name | San José Name (1790s) |
|---|---|---|
| Haawo? | Akäbäk: raccoon<br>Ts?uts?u: coatimundi | Jague |
| Kasyho? | Ma?ax: spider monkey<br>Ba?ats: howler monkey | |
| Keho? | Yuk: white-tailed deer<br>Keh: mule deer | |
| Kobaho? | Chilu: quail | |
| Koho? | K?ek?en: white-lipped peccary<br>Kitam: collared peccary | Cobog |
| Miso? | Mo?: macaw<br>Ka?cho: parrot | |
| Nahwahto? | K?ambul: curassow<br>Koox: wild turkey | Naguate |
| Nistisyaho? | Hale: paca<br>Tsup: prairie dog | |
| Puko? | Balum: jaguar<br>Chäk Balum: puma | Puc |
| Taxo? | Sa?hol: badger | |
| Uuko? | Uuk: dove<br>Ts?ul: dove | |
| Witso? | Hunk?uk: eagle | |

José was abandoned in 1807 these people disappear from the historical record. Where the Cobog, Naguate, Jague, and Puc families moved when they left San José cannot be determined, but there are many accounts of contact with Yucatec-Lacandon families in western Guatemala and eastern Chiapas in the early nineteenth century. The final important lesson to be derived from the story of the mission at San José is that the Lacandon of the time, although living deep in the forests, were hardly isolated. To the contrary, there was an active exchange of people and products between the Lacandon and Spanish frontier towns. This exchange of materials and ideas accelerated in the nineteenth century, especially after the wars of independence from Spain when the new Mexican and Guatemalan republics began to send government officials, missionaries, settlers, and businessmen into the vast tracts of forest that covered their common border.

## Lacandon in the Nineteenth Century

It is impossible to say exactly how and when the ancestors of the modern Lacandon moved into eastern Chiapas. Clearly, by the eighteenth century Yucatec-speaking Lacandon were scattered throughout western Guatemala and eastern Chiapas, where they moved through the forests, ignored political boundaries, and shunned unwanted contact at will. However, other than the documents relating to the community of San José, little is known of these people or how they lived until European explorers began traveling through the lowlands and Capuchin monks undertook missions into the Petén in the 1850s and 1860s. It is the ethnographic accounts written by these people who give us the best look at Lacandon life in the second half of the nineteenth century.

Today, there are two distinct Lacandon societies, the Northern Lacandon, who live primarily in the communities of Mensäbäk and Nahá, and the Southern Lacandon, most of whom live in the community of Lacanha Chan Sayab just a few miles from the Classic Period Maya site of Bonampak. The two groups are culturally and linguistically distinct, although there is an enclave of Northern Lacandon in Lacanha. These three communities, however, are an artifact of twentieth-century immigration and land distribution policies, and the formation of the Montes Azules Biosphere Reserve in 1971. In the nineteenth century, the Lacandon were scattered throughout the forests of Chiapas and western Guatemala in small settlements and extended family compounds.

In the first half of the nineteenth century, at the same time that logging companies began to focus their attention on extracting wood from the tropical forests, European and American adventurers began to explore the jungle and encountered Lacandon camps. In the 1830s and 1840s, John L. Stevens and Frederick Catherwood explored the ruins of Palenque and met some Lacandon. In Palenque, they heard that several years before an Irishman named William Beanham had lived with the Lacandon for nearly a year. While preparing for his return to the jungle, Beanham had been murdered and his account of his experiences destroyed (Nations 1984:29).

In the 1850s, Capuchin monks worked in a Lacandon community at Petexbatum, near the site of Seibal on the Pasión River. A few miles dowstream from this community was another on Lake Izan, visited by Karl Sapper in 1891.

In 1865, exploring along the Pasión River, C. H. Berendt encountered friendly Lacandon, who helped guide his excursions through the forest. Berendt observed that these "eastern Lacandon lived in small palm huts, consisting of little more than a roof," and made their living by farming, hunting, and fishing (1867:425). He also wrote that these Lacandon had been baptized by Catholic missionaries but still practiced polygyny and adhered to "their old heathen worship" although he does not describe their religious practices (1867:425). Berendt also mentions western Lacandon, who he said lived far from the settlements of whites and were feared by the Lacandon he stayed with, undoubtedly referring to Lacandon settlements farther west in Chiapas.

Traveling through parts of Mexico and Central America in the 1870s, John Boddam-Whetham heard stories about the Lacandon and came across a Lacandon camp. Later, in Tenosique, he was told that small parties of Lacandon occasionally came to town to exchange vanilla, cacao, and tobacco for salt, cotton, and firearms (1877:22). I heard the same story over a century later in life histories I recorded with elderly Lacandon.

In the 1880s, government surveyors attempting to demarcate the boundary between Mexico and Guatemala found that the proposed boundary ran through several small groups of Yucatec Lacandon (Hellmuth 1970:78 cited in Nations 1979:99). During this same period, A. P. Maudsley encountered a Lacandon community near the mouth of the Lacantun River and another near Yaxchilan (1889–1902: pt.3, 40).

In 1891 and 1894, Karl Sapper visited Lacandon families in Chiapas and on Lake Izan in Guatemala. Seven years later, Teobert Maler, who was searching for ancient Maya ruins along the Usumacinta River, visited a Lacandon settlement at Lake Bolonchac to the east of Yaxchilan and took the first known photograph of a Lacandon (1903:201). Additionally, Maler reported a settlement down the Usumacinta River near the site of Piedras Negras. Excavations at Piedras Negras have also uncovered Lacandon-style incense burners in the ruins (Thompson 1977:15).

What was Lacandon life like in the 1890s? Berendt (1867:425) claims the western Lacandon spoke Chol, but Sapper (1897) wrote that all Lacandon in his day spoke Yucatec Maya and that the Chol-speaking western Lacandon were extinct. All visitors to the area commented on the Lacandon's bow and arrows, but despite the fact that he saw Lacandon with steel machetes and axes, Sapper still considered them to be a Stone-Age culture. Because Sapper saw only small maize and bean fields in forest clearings and did not encounter Lacandon clearing fields, he speculated that the Lacandon subsisted primarily by hunting and fishing. He believed they only farmed areas where windfalls had made natural clearings in the forest (1897). However, other visitors to Lacandon camps typically comment on their farming skill and mention cornfields and fruit trees.

Virtually all visitors who mention the dress of the Lacandon say it was simple, with men wearing a long shirt and women wearing gowns of coarse fabric over skirts. Both men and women went barefoot. Men wore their hair long, falling down over their shoulders. Women bound their hair in a ponytail that hung down their backs and which they decorated with parrot feathers. Both men and women, Sapper observed, wore necklaces of snail shells and beads.

Lacandon homes were simple, rectangular, one-room affairs, with a low thatched roof for privacy. Similarly, when allowed to see the ceremonial structures, visitors' descriptions typically sound much like those of a contemporary Lacandon god house: low thatched roof and hanging shelves on the western side of the structure on which were placed incense burners, which Sapper described as "clay bowls with face masks" (1897).

Sapper visited a Lacandon settlement on Lake Izan in western Guatemala in 1891 and a second community on Lake Pethá in eastern Chiapas in 1894. He related that in both places the people were shy and gentle and that they would abandon their homes and move deeper into the jungle when contacted by outsiders. Sapper said that Lacandon of eastern Chiapas were large and powerful, and that their hunting bows were almost exactly the height of the men who carried them. Although he only saw a few families, it was his opinion that polygyny "prevailed" among them, but he commented that he noticed few children.

Sapper said that the Lacandon would not discuss their religious customs with him but then went on to describe things he had heard of their ritual practices. He said that they painted themselves for their ceremonies and prepared a fermented mead called *balché.* He also stated that Lacandon made pilgrimages to a site he called *Menche Tunamit* (today's Yaxchilan) where they left "sacrificial bowls" probably incense burners. Finally, Sapper believed the Lacandon were of special importance because, by investigating their customs, "there must still fall many a revealing light on the mysterious mythology and remarkable customs of the ancient civilized nations of the Maya" (1897:264).

The idea that the Lacandon were somehow linked to the civilization of the ancient Maya was common at the turn of the century. Sapper's notion has proved to be a popular and enduring theme with authors writing about the Lacandon. Even today after one hundred years of ethnographic research, the Lacandon are still romanticized as the last remnants of the ancient Maya. However, as the preceeding descriptions show, the nineteeth-century Lacandon were in constant contact with people from outside the forest and were actively trading for metal tools and other forms of modern technology. Even their farming practices, which Nations and Nigh (1980:2) suppose to be similar to that of the ancient Maya, underwent dramatic changes in the nineteenth century. In his excavations of nineteenth-century Lacandon settlements Palka found evidence that the Lacandon of that day were cultivating a variety of Old World plants such as bananas, oranges, watermelons, mangos, and sugarcane (1998:469). As their desire for goods such as steel machetes and axes, salt, ceramic vessels, and cloth grew, the Lacandon's need to produce products for trade increased. It was tools such as axes and machetes that helped them intensify agricultural production to produce crops for trade. Lacandon agricultural practices are efficient, productive, and exceptionally well suited to their environment. However, as the preceding discussion makes clear, even their form of subsistence has not remained unchanged from ancient Maya times.

The most comprehensive descriptions of Lacandon life at the close of the nineteenth century and in the first decade of the twentieth century come from the German explorer Teobert Maler and Harvard anthropologist Alfred Tozzer. In August 1898, in the midst of the rainy season, Teobert Maler set out to discover the forgotten Lake of Pethá, apparently unaware that Sapper had been there four years earlier. We are fortunate that he was not aware of Sapper's excursion to Lake Pethá, for Maler left us a detailed first-person description of nineteenth-century Lacandon life. Starting at the small town of La Reforma on August 27, Maler traveled south following the Chocolha River (a tributary of the Usumacinta) which he finally crossed on September 3, 1898. A short distance from their crossing place Maler and his companions found a shelter, cooking hut, and several hunting trails. Maler followed a trail that led in a southerly direction for most of the day and finally came to a *milpa* in the middle of the forest.

Cautiously descending a hill, Maler's party suddenly came to the shore of Lake Pethá where they found three dugout canoes. As they made camp for the night they spotted a canoe with two men passing into a cove on the other side of the lake. The next day they borrowed the canoes and crossed the lake, discovering an inlet where they found several more canoes. Securing the dugouts, Maler and his men followed a path inland and after hiking about thirty minutes they found a large *milpa*. Walking through maize, banana and papaya trees, and sugarcane they saw a cluster of houses that had been hastily abandoned. Maler took the opportunity to examine the houses and their contents in great detail. He reported that the houses were made of poles roofed with palm leaves and filled with household implements. He found clay cooking pots and water jars, a large metate (grinding stone), and net bags hanging from the rafters filled with drinking gourds and bowls. Bundles of tobacco leaves also hung from the rafters along with several sets of bows and arrows. There were gourd bowls of seed corn, wax, and spindles of cotton thread. In one of the small huts nearby they found a beehive made from a large gourd, pear-shaped birdcages made of plaited vines, and a variety of animal skins. The compound also had a ceremonial hut, apparently the largest structure in the compound. Inside, Maler found and photographed incense burners like those he had encountered in the temples at Yaxchilan. Though the whole compound was located in the middle of a *milpa*, the space between structures had been planted with flowers and herbs.

On September 5, Maler and his men reconnoitered the entire lake. They found and copied a series of rock paintings on an exposed rock face above the water. These paintings allow us to conclusively identify Maler's location and Lake Pethá; the paintings are on a cliff overlooking Lake Itsanok?uh near the Lacandon community of Mensäbäk. I visited this Lacandon cave shrine on the lake in 1980 and saw these paintings on the return trip to Mensäbäk.

Returning to trace the paintings on September 6, Maler finally had his first face-to-face encounter with a Lacandon. As he was tracing the rock drawings he was approached by a canoe carrying a Lacandon man, his wife, and three children. The man was greatly agitated at the presence of Maler's party and called for them to leave, saying: "No hombre—quítate de ahi—es mi santo—es el Cristo-María de nosotros—cuidado hombre . . . " (Maler 1903:32).

Maler calmed the man, who was named Chan K?in, and explained that he was there to visit and trade. He promptly bought Chan K?in's bows and arrows for two pesos. Returning to shore Maler and his men followed Chan K?in and his family for several hours along difficult jungle trails. They finally arrived at Chan K?in's compound where he lived with his brother-in-law, who gave his name as Max (the *onen ma?ax*). Max agreed to provide them with food, and although Max was not enthusiastic about their presence, Maler and his men made plans to return the next day. The following day, Maler once again crossed the lake to "observe the habits and customs of the Indians and to take some small photographs" (1903:34). He also distributed gourdfuls of salt, knives, and fishhooks to the men and kerchiefs, mirrors, and earrings to the women in exchange for permission to take their photographs. Maler described the men at Pethá as wearing a shirt-like garment of strong coarse cotton that reached down to their calves. The women wore a skirt of a similar material and a long blouse over the skirt. Looking at one of his photographs (Figure 1.1), one can see that men wore their hair long and uncut about their shoulders and women wore ponytails which they decorated with bird feathers. They also wore bunches of seed necklaces.

From Maler's description we know that the people he visited at Pethá built their homes in their *milpa*. They lived in large thatched roof houses with dirt floors that were surrounded by smaller structures for cooking and other household activities.

**FIGURE 1.1**     The Lacandon at Lake Pethá, photographed by Teobert Maler, 1898.

There was also a god house, or ceremonial hut, in the compound. Apparently, these compounds were widely dispersed. Maler claimed that each family lived about an hour's journey from anyone else, although he didn't visit any other compounds to verify the accuracy of this observation. Maler also looked for examples of glyphs in the compound but found nothing that resembled ancient Maya writing. He also claimed the locals had no knowledge of ruins in the area, which was probably not true; the nearest ruins are Palenque, Yaxchilan, Bonampak, Seibal, and Lacanha, all of which were within a two-day walk from his location.

 Maler provided a detailed description of many of the material items he found in the Lacandon camp at Pethá. The people in the compound headed by the man Maler called Max slept in hammocks knotted from agave fiber. They wore garments of rough homespun cotton, used gourd bowls and plates, cooked in clay pots, and hung objects from woven net bags and baskets from the rafters of their thatched huts. But what can we infer about the lives of the Lacandon men and women he met from this catalog of material life?

Maler's account deals mostly with the men. They fished and hunted with bows and arrows with which Maler apparently was impressed, as he bought or traded for several sets. A whole page of Maler's account is devoted to a description of bows and arrows. He also described how Lacandon men fashioned projectile points by splitting off flakes of chert with a section of deer horn or from pieces of broken glass. Maler listed the five kinds of fish he said Lacandon men told him they took from the lake. Noted only in passing were the large *milpas* where he saw bananas, papaya, sugar cane, and "luxuriant corn" (1903:26). Though these fields must have provided the bulk of the Lacandons' food, they were apparently just part of the landscape as far as Maler was concerned because he did not describe them in any detail. Maler also did not report on whether men or women were working in the *milpas* he passed through. Finally, Maler had the opportunity to watch the men conduct part of a religious ceremony in which they wore red headbands and prayed in the distinctive nasalized monotone voice that Lacandon men adopt to pray.

Maler did not discuss the activities of Lacandon women in any detail, which is not surprising. When he was in Max's compound the women probably stayed in the background, carefully watching the stranger but letting their husbands and sons deal directly with him. Maler commented on the rough cotton garments he saw people wearing and on one woman who "obstinately" refused to sell him her loom, so we know that at least some Lacandon women spun cotton thread which they wove into fabric for garments. He also mentions seeing *manos* and metates and women making tortillas, so it is a good guess that the women spent significant time grinding corn and cooking. Unfortunately, Maler wrote nothing more on the activities of Lacandon women.

In contrast to the general opinion that the Lacandon were wild and uncivilized, the people of Pethá were apparently used to making commercial transactions at lumber camps and villages on the periphery of the forest. Maler says that when he departed Pethá on September 12, 1898, several Lacandon men accompanied them on the two-day journey north to a lumber camp called Tinieblas. There the men purchased various items before departing for home early the following morning.

# Lacandon in the Twentieth Century

As we have seen, both Sapper and Maler wrote brief descriptions of Lacandon life as they saw it, but their real interests were in discovering and mapping Maya ruins. The first attempt to present a comprehensive picture of the Lacandon Maya was by Harvard anthropologist Alfred Tozzer, who observed life in a Lacandon community in 1903 and again in 1904.

Alfred Marston Tozzer, or Don Alfredo as he was known by the Lacandon, studied Maya in the Yucatan before traveling to Chiapas in February of 1903. Tozzer sailed up the Usumacinta River to the town of Tenosique. From Tenosique he sailed upriver for three more days to the Hacienda Santa Margarita, where he hired horses and a guide to continue his journey to Lake Pethá to revisit the people that Maler had contacted five years previously. He made first contact with the Lacandon on March 1, 1903. Here is how Tozzer described his first sight of a Lacandon:

> Don Rafael was a little in advance of me and as I turned in the path I saw him talking with the most curious looking man. His hair was long and unkept hanging over his shoulders. He wore a sort of poncho-like affair which hung just below the knees and this was his only dress. A scanty and straggly beard made his appearance all the more strange and out of the ordinary. It did not take me long to find out who he was for when I addressed some words in Maya to him, his face lighted up with a smile and I knew I had found my first Carib or Maya of Chiapas. (Letter of March 1, 1903)

Tozzer settled at a compound of three Lacandon families headed by a man he called García, who resided some distance from the lake. Tozzer was allowed to move into an abandoned hut and he began a four-week stay in 1903, returning for another six weeks in 1904. Like others before him, Tozzer's primary interests were in Lacandon religion and he was able to witness two incense burner renewal ceremonies, one of the most important of Lacandon rites. In one report, he described Lacandon religious practices as "clearly survivals of the ancient culture" (1903:47). However, like Maler's experience, Tozzer's attempts to find survivals of ancient Maya culture baffled his Lacandon hosts. They did not recognize anything in the Maya codices Tozzer had brought to show them.

Although Tozzer said the Lacandon avoided contact with Mexicans, reading his letters from the field it is clear that the people living in this house compound were not isolated in the forest. The settlement was near one of the principal trails used by the Compañía Mexicana Sud Oriental to supply the men in its logging camps scattered through the forest and the Lacandon traded bananas and tobacco in the camps for salt (1978:33). Additionally, the Lacandon settlement was apparently quite close to a logging camp because Tozzer had his camp cook buy many of their supplies from the camp stores in the *monterías*. Tozzer also mentioned that a few Lacandon had cut their hair and adopted a Mexican lifestyle (1978:34). This is further evidence of the variety of ways in which Lacandon at the time were attempting to integrate their lives into the wider world around them.

Tozzer's 1907 book, *A Comparative Study of the Maya and Lacandones*, provides the most comprehensive look at Lacandon life at the turn of the twentieth century. However, he focused most of his time and attention on observing and recording the religious rituals conducted by Lacandon men because he believed he was witnessing a survival of the ancient Maya religion (1978:79). Because he was so busy trying to sneak peeks of activities conducted in the god house, Tozzer wrote little of the everyday lives of men and women as those lives flowed around him. I am especially sensitive to this fact now, in large part, because I made the same mistake almost one hundred years later in my book *Life, Ritual, and Religion among the Lacandon Maya* (1990). Like Tozzer, my own interests were primarily in religion. Because I was single and I spent most of my time with Lacandon men, Lacandon women are virtually absent from this work. My own interests blinded me to the activity of women that was going on all around me. Being male and single it would have been difficult for me to spend as much time with Lacandon women as I did with men, but the sad truth is that I never much thought about it.

After Tozzer, little work was conducted among the Lacandon until Jacques Soustelle and the archeologist Franz Blom began working in the forests of southeastern Chiapas in the 1930s. Soustelle wrote a report of his visits to three Lacandon compounds which he described as being between the El Real a La Mar, Jatate, Lacantun, and Usumacinta Rivers (1933:153). One of these compounds was at a site he called Lake Peljá (probably

Pethá) and the other two compounds were at Jetjá, a place visited by Franz Blom a decade later. Soustelle counted thirty-three people in the various households but not everyone would show themselves. He guessed that in the combined households there were eleven men, twelve women, and ten children, and estimated their ages (1933:156).

Unlike most visitors who romanticized the Lacandon they met, Soustelle commented unfavorably on several aspects of their lives. Although he went on to write a doctoral thesis about the Lacandon (1937) and published articles on them for almost twenty years, Soustelle apparently did not have a high opinion of the people he met. Moira Di Mauro-Jackson, who helped me translate his work, noticed that many of the terms he used in reference to the Lacandon in his 1933 report are typically used by speakers of French to refer to animals.

Because he saw few children Soustelle concluded that their fertility was faulty (*"Il est donc évident que la fécondité est faible"*; 1933:156). Soustelle blamed this situation on the fact that younger men were with older women (although the older women he saw were probably the widowed mothers or mothers-in-law of the men he met, not their wives). He also found Lacandon culture lacking because they had not domesticated pigs like the Tzeltal Maya communities he visited (1933:160).

Typical of the anthropology of his time, Soustelle tried to take physical measurements of the people he interviewed but many refused. However, Soustelle had an eye for detail and his report contains a variety of details about Lacandon life in the 1930s that few other reports mention. For example, Soustelle is the first ethnographer I have found who mentioned the Lacandon raising chickens (1933:160). He is one of the few ethnographers who discussed the work that women were doing. Soustelle described how women started cooking fires by striking flint against a piece of iron (1933:162) and how metates were obtained in the town of Tenosique. He noted that women spun cotton thread and saw women weaving on both set frame and back strap looms (1933:166). He noted that some households were polygynous and that a few men had taken child brides (1933:157). Soustelle also described their *milpas*, the food they ate, their clothes, and the construction of their houses. He mentions the game men hunted and describes how men went bow fishing. And of course, Soustelle devoted a great deal of attention to Lacandon religion (1933, 1935, 1959). Unlike other visitors he also recognized that the people in the communities he visited had a variety of contacts with outsiders and he describes interactions between Northern and Southern Lacandon, Tzeltal Maya, and Mexican workers in the lumber camps (1933:179).

In the 1940s, Franz Blom and his wife, Gertrude Duby-Blom, traveled extensively in the Lacandon Jungle. They found that the largest Lacandon settlements, or *caribales,* were concentrated in three areas (see Map 1.1). These were the Cedro-Lacanha group living near the Lacanha River and the ruins of Bonampak, the Jatate group living farther south along the Jatate River, and the northern group (including Maler and Tozzer's Pethá families) living between the Rio Santa Cruz and Rio Santo Domingo (Duby and Blom 1969:276). Several years earlier, Blom had conducted a census of Lacandon families and listed the places where he had contacted them (1944:60). That list, reproduced in Table 1.2, demonstrates that the scattered settlement patterns of the nineteenth century were still in practice and that the Lacandon population was fairly small. A note following Blom's list says that there

TABLE 1.2    Location of Lacandon Families in 1944

| Name | Location | Population |
|---|---|---|
| El Desempeño | Usumacinta River (Guatemala) | 1 man, 2 women |
| El Cedro | Chiapas | 7 men, 14 women, some children |
| Arroyo Jetjá | Chiapas | 9 men, with women and children |
| Arroyo Arena | Chiapas | 1 man |
| Arroyo Chocolja | Chiapas | 4 men |
| Santo Domingo | Chiapas | 3 men, 4 women, and some children |
| San Quintín | Chiapas (Jataté River) | 6 men with women and children |

were two more groups of Lacandon in the *Zona de Zendales* near the Lacantun River and that he was almost certain there were no more than 250 living Lacandon.

Scholars and travelers have consistently romanticized the Lacandon as an artifact of the past at the mercy of forces who have invaded their jungle and disrupted their lives. Like those before them, Duby and Blom mistakenly wrote that the Lacandon had resisted all attempts to change them since Father Calderón's failed mission at San José de Gracia Real in the 1790s. The villains who had brought evil into Eden in Duby and Blom's tale were the lumber companies who set up logging camps in the second half of the nineteenth century (1969:277).

It is true that the European and North American market for tropical hardwoods provided an incentive for the exploitation of the resources of the lowland forests, and that the men who worked in the *monterías* were agents of change in Lacandon society. However, as we have seen in this chapter, the depiction of the Lacandon as helpless children of the forest does not present an accurate picture of their interactions with outsiders. Judging from the accounts in Father Calderón's reports of San José in the 1790s, the Lacandon built the mission at a site of their choosing and established a lucrative trade with the people in Palenque, exchanging bows and arrows and tobacco for products such as steel tools and manufactured cloth. That San José was settled primarily as a commercial venture in Lacandon eyes is indicated by the fact that they continued to worship their Maya gods in a temple they built at the edge of the community. Some Lacandon men even married women in Palenque.

San José was abandoned in less than two decades, but the Lacandon did not disappear. Although their contact with outsiders was intermittent, there is a clear record of contact between Lacandon, lumbermen, missionaries, and other visitors throughout the nineteenth century. Archeological excavations of nineteenth-century Lacandon settlements show clearly that the Lacandon maintained commercial exchange networks like those of the people of San José. Excavations at the nineteenth-century Lacandon site of El Caobal in the Pasión River area found that about 50 percent of the artifacts uncovered were of nonindigenous origin. These included fragments of a Blue Willow–pattern serving plate from Belize, steel machete, scissors, file, steel pot, blown glass bottles, and other whiteware ceramics, in addition to traditional Lacandon ceramics and chert projectile points and blades (Palka and Olivares 1992:4; Palka 1998:464).

Maler and Tozzer's descriptions of life in the Pethá region support the archeological evidence. Lacandon families were clearly engaging in a variety of commercial transactions with men in the lumber camps and people in nearby towns. The turn-of-the-century observations of Maler and Tozzer were confirmed for me in interviews with Lacandon elders who described making trips to the town of Tenosique on foot, packing bundles of bows and arrows to trade for salt, machetes, and bullets.

Duby and Blom wrote during a time when the Lacandon's pattern of interaction with outsiders once again was beginning to change. Before World War II, Lacandon communication with the outside world was largely on their terms—at the times they chose for the reasons they chose. With no roads and few trails through the forest outsiders could be avoided. If one needed salt, bullets, a new ax, or cloth, it was a simple matter to visit the nearest *montería* or town. However, after World War II, the Mexican government's land reform policies opened up areas of the forest to colonization and the industrial exploitation of the forest intensified. Thus the nature of the interactions between the Lacandon and those from outside the forest began to change. Encouraged by the passage of agrarian reform laws, new immigrants—Tzeltal and Tzotzil Maya from the highlands of Chiapas—moved from the highlands, down the Ocosingo Valley and into the Lacandon Jungle. Tzeltal from Ocosingo, for example, founded the community of Lacandon just a few miles from Nahá and were given ownership of the land in 1954 (Arizpe, Paz, and Velázquez 1996:25–26).

Outside pressure on the Lacandon also was exerted by Chol speakers from around Palenque who moved into the forest. Like the Tzeltal, the Chol immigrants are descended from Indians who were forcibly removed from the jungle in the sixteenth century, and since that time have toiled as laborers on sugarcane, coffee, and cattle *fincas*. When these plantations were broken up in the 1930s, the Chol received small parcels of land to farm. But the amount of land was inadequate for the growing population, and families began to migrate to the eastern forest where they raised corn, coffee, and cattle, as they had when working as debt peons on lowland plantations. In the 1960s, as immigration into the jungle increased, Lacandon settlements visited by Duby and Blom in the 1930s and 1940s disappeared. In particular, the lives of the Lacandon in the area of the Jatate River, in locations such as Puna, Capulín, El Censo, and Monte Líbano, were disrupted by the influx of Tzeltal immigrants from the Ocosingo Valley. Several Lacandon families moved eastward into the forest and relocated near Lakes Mensäbäk and Itzanok⁷uh (near the turn-of-the-century settlement called Pethá) and founded the settlement of Mensäbäk.

In the 1970s, the agrarian policies of President Luis Echeverría encouraged the settlement of the forest in eastern Chiapas. Landless peasants from northern Mexican states such as Sonora and Chihuahua were given land grants and resettled in the Lacandon forest (Arizpe et al., 1996:28). The traditional Lacandon settlement pattern of dispersed, extended family compounds, shifted to larger communities such as Lacanha Chan Sayab and Nahá. At the same time they were encouraging immigration into the forest, the Mexican government proposed to slow deforestation in the Lacandon Jungle by creating the *Zona Lacandona*, a forest reserve. Part of this plan was resettling almost 6,000 Tzeltal and Chol Maya into new settlements outside the zone's boundaries. At the same time numerous Lacandon families were encouraged to move into the zone, and as a group the Lacandon were given a grant of 614,321 hectares of land. Unfortunately, one result of the resettlement policy was that it created tremendous resentment toward the Lacandon. Those other Maya who had moved into the forest to farm in the previous decades and then were forcibly resettled, understandably felt that in favoring the Lacandon the government had treated them unfairly.

Although I did not realize it at the time, of all the projects started in Chiapas in the 1970s, road construction probably had the farthest-reaching consequences. As discussed earlier in this chapter, the Lacandon have never been completely isolated from the outside world. Like the modern population, the eighteenth-century Lacandon conducted business with the people of Palenque. In the early part of this century, trading of bows and arrows, tobacco, and honey was common. These items were bartered for other subsistence items, in particular, salt and metal tools. However, before the road, Lacandon commercial transactions were limited by geography and lack of transportation. If a man wanted to sell bows and arrows, he packed as many as he could carry on his back and walked to the nearest large towns of Ocosingo, Tenosique, or Palenque. These trips required a couple of days of hard hiking through forested mountainous terrain, so contact with the outside world was intermittent. With the road and a community truck, travel to Palenque became easier, and many men began to make bows and arrows as a commercial enterprise. Additionally, the government's investment in roads encouraged travel and tourism in Chiapas, in particular linking Palenque and San Cristobal through Ocosingo. So the effect of the roads into the forest was twofold. First, roads helped speed the colonization of the forest and its subsequent deforestation. Second, the roads facilitated the Lacandons' access to tourists and for the first time made tourism a viable alternative to farming. This process has had dramatic consequences for Lacandon society and will be discussed in greater detail later in Chapter 4.

## Lacandon 1980–2000

The last two decades of Lacandon history are the principal focus of this book. I arrived in Nahá in the summer of 1980 at a time when the economic situation in Chiapas was about to change dramatically. In 1981, oil accounted for 68.7 percent of Mexico's total exports (Cancian 1992:32). However, a decade of oil-fueled economic prosperity in Mexico came to an abrupt end when the world oil market weakened in 1981. The Mexican oil economy collapsed, encouraging a new emphasis on the importance of tourism. Since they supported themselves through *milpa* farming, the scaling back of government programs was not traumatic for most Lacandon, in particular, as households received royalty payments for lumber contracts let by the Mexican government. The economic crash in Mexico, although devastating to Mexican citizens, was a boon to the tourist industry. The devaluations of the Mexican peso in the 1980s made traveling in Mexico cheap and the large Indian population of Chiapas made it an attractive destination for European tourists. As the number of tourists flocking to visit the ruins of Palenque and Bonampak increased, Lacandon men produced more tourist goods to meet the demand and earn easy cash.

For someone like me, who enjoyed a life paced by the rising and setting of the sun, sitting around the kitchen hearth, and working by candlelight, some of the most startling changes in Lacandon society occurred in the 1990s. Electric service came to Nahá in 1993, with television and satellite dishes following almost immediately afterward. The Zapatista uprising began in January 1994 and was quickly followed by the militarization of the *Zona Lacandona*. A school was built in 1995, and a murder in the spring of 1999 led to the construction of a jail. In May of 2001 I discovered that there was a satellite telephone system in Nahá, and that a few men were communicating through email. Whereas economic changes have encouraged a return to the land in the highlands of Chiapas, since the 1980s many Lacandon men have made a large-scale move from subsistence farming to the full-time sale of crafts, and hired Tzeltal Maya to grow corn for them. In addition, conflicts with squatter communities of Zapatista supporters over land rights have escalated. Finally, practitioners of the old non-Christian religion are now almost completely gone. The old religion has not so much died as faded away. For two decades after the Protestant conversion of the other communities, the non-Christian religious traditions held on in Nahá. Today, with the death and failing health of the communities' religious leaders, few young men have bothered to continue the old rituals. There has not yet been widespread conversion to Christianity in Nahá as in the other communities. Instead, men have simply ceased to practice any religion at all.

The last two decades have been a time of tremendous change in Lacandon society. The shift from a society based on subsistence agriculture to a mixed economy based on agriculture and tourism has started profound changes in Lacandon society, the results of which may not be fully felt for decades. The social and material structure of Lacandon life is changing just as the ecology of the forest in which they live is in transition due to settlement and development. Work, gender relations, family structure, and material life have all shifted since Tozzer camped out in Jose Bol García's storage hut. Today I feel my role is to document those changes as best I can. My students often ask me if I am saddened by what has happened to the Lacandon in the last decades. I answer that it is true that Lacandon society as I experienced it in 1980 is largely gone. But then the life in the United States that I lived in 1980 is gone too. Whether I think the changes are good or bad is irrelevant. I do not know enough to make those kinds of conclusions for my Lacandon friends. It is their life to live, not mine.

# CHAPTER

## 2 Reconstructing the Traditional Lacandon

In Chapter 1, I provided a brief history of the Lacandon in Chiapas, described the numerous contacts with the Yucatec-speaking Lacandon starting in 1790, and presented an overview of what life was like for the Lacandon of the eighteenth, nineteenth, and twentieth centuries. In particular, I showed that three popular myths about the Lacandon—that they are the direct descendants of the builders of the great Maya sites such as Palenque and Yaxchilan, that the Lacandon have preserved the ancient culture because they were isolated from the rest of the world, and that because of this isolation, Lacandon culture today is a window into ancient Maya life—are all untrue when one studies the historical record.

Friends who have read early drafts of this book have argued that my work on Lacandon Maya religion proves that there are links between the Lacandon and ancient Maya, and in a general sense I suppose that is true. I have found some elements of Lacandon ritual symbolism (McGee 1990, 1998), cosmology (McGee and Reilly, 1997), and mythology (McGee 1997a) that are similar to those depicted in ancient Maya art and chronicled by the Spaniards. But the assumption that looking at contemporary Lacandon society is like looking through a window into the ancient Maya past is true only in the sense that looking at all Maya groups is, in a manner of speaking, looking at the past. The Spaniards' conquest of the Maya devastated sixteenth-century Maya society. All elements of Maya culture were disrupted, from their social and political order to settlement patterns, religious beliefs, and food production. Maya societies today are descended from that awful period of political upheaval and social devastation.

The Lacandon are different only in that they apparently never lived under direct Spanish control. But it is wrong to assume they survived untouched and unchanged in the forest. Historical and archeological evidence indicates otherwise.

In this chapter I would like to discuss three topics that can provide insights that are of critical importance to the discipline of anthropology, as well as understanding the Lacandon. The first issue is the question of how to define the Lacandon, or any other ethnic group. The second notion deals with defining what is a traditional behavior or lifestyle. A great deal has been written about "traditional" Lacandon lifestyles when in fact very little information is available about Lacandon life before the middle of the twentieth century. The two obvious questions that arise are what is meant by the term *traditional* and how does one know something is traditional?

The third issue relates to the second, and is of even greater consequence to the study of anthropology. This is the notion of what I call the generic ethnic group. It is common in virtually all ethnographic writing to make general statements about a people. An example from my book on Lacandon religion is, "The Lacandon believe that red is a favorite color of the gods because it is associated with blood" (1990:89). The literature on the Lacandon is full of generic statements about them as if they were a monolithic entity. However, as the historical overview in Chapter 1 demonstrates, the Lacandon are an ethnically and geographically diverse group of people who until the 1960s lived primarily in isolated multigeneration house compounds. Because the majority of Lacandon have lived anonymously and unnoticed by outsiders, even today I think it is difficult to make generalizations that accurately apply to all Lacandon. In fact, for any but the most general of statements, I can probably find Lacandon individuals or a family who contradict the observation. All I can really say for certain about the Lacandon applies only to those families I have interviewed and observed. Thus, referring again to my observation about the color red and blood, I actually have no idea what the majority of Lacandon believe is a favorite color of the gods. I know that the half dozen men I asked in 1981 and 1982 believed that red was a favorite color of the gods. That observation may be held by most Lacandon, but I don't know because I haven't consulted most Lacandon on the subject. It would be more accurate to say that in 1982, the group of men who practiced rituals in Chan K?in Viejo's god house agreed that red was a favorite color of the gods because it was associated with blood.

My point is that the Lacandon as a generic entity are a creation of those who write about them. There are six hundred or so Lacandon individuals. What they do is determined largely by whether they are men or women, children or adults, and married or single. I have come to realize that for the sake of ethnographic accuracy, and to be fair to the people I write about, I need to be exceedingly careful about the statements I make about them and to incorporate the factors of gender, age, and marital status in my observations.

## Who Is Lacandon?

The stereotypical image of a Lacandon presented to a visitor to Chiapas is that of a man with long hair hanging down to his shoulders, wearing a long white smock called a *xikul* and typically holding a bow and arrow. This stereotype is so pervasive that I don't believe I have ever seen a poster or magazine cover showing a Lacandon woman, many of whom wear makeup and dress in current Mexican fashion, or a Lacandon man with short hair, wearing pants and a shirt. In fact, some visitors are distressed when they pay for an expedition to observe the exotic Lacandon and find people with short hair, wearing T-shirts and watching *telenovelas* (Mexican soap operas) on television. That is not what the tour operators have led them to expect.

The Lacandon categorize human beings into four groups. Lacandon call themselves *Hach Winik,* or "real people." Other Indians are called *kah* which is derived from the word *kahal,* meaning "town." Foreign men are labeled *tsur* and foreign women *xunaan.* Outsiders to the Lacandon Jungle, Mexicans and tourists alike, have typically identified the definitive characteristics of a Lacandon man as his long uncut hair, knee-length white smock, and non-Christian religious beliefs. I always assumed that a Lacandon identity was signified by a person's long dark hair, dark skin and eyes, and speaking of *hach t?an,* or "real language." However, none of these criteria are significant to the Lacandon. When it occurred to me to ask a wide sample of Lacandon men and women how they knew whether someone was Lacandon, I got a completely different answer.

To all Lacandon I have quizzed on this issue, the single diagnostic characteristic of Lacandoness is that one's father is Lacandon. If I married a Lacandon women and had a child who had dark hair, dark eyes, and spoke *hach t'an*, that child would be a *tsur* or *xunaan*. On the other hand, if a woman marries a Lacandon man and bears a blonde-haired, blue-eyed baby with fair skin, the child is considered Lacandon. Thus for the sake of ethnographic accuracy, note that none of the characteristics of traditional Lacandon life as it has been defined by two centuries of visitors to the forest is the least bit significant to the Lacandon's concept of themselves as a people. Those who have written about Lacandon society have typically defined the Lacandon purely on the criteria they saw as significant. If in two hundred years I was the first person to ask a Lacandon how they defined themselves, what then of the popular notion of the traditional Lacandon?

## What Is a Traditional Lacandon?

As I discussed in Chapter 1, writers have assumed the Lacandon were a traditional people since the mid-nineteenth century, but they expended little time in defining what they meant by the term *traditional*. A number of writers have popularized the idea that the Lacandon were a window onto the ancient Maya past. Numerous examples of how different aspects of Lacandon life have been assumed to be related to the ancient Maya, or at least traditional, are found in works throughout this century, even (I am embarrassed to say) in my own work. Teobert Maler (1898) hoped to find evidence of hieroglyphic writing among the Lacandon. Harvard anthropologist Alfred Tozzer's 1907 monograph attempted to link the Lacandon with the ancient Maya. David Amram published an account of his visit to a Lacandon community in which he speculated they were the "last surviving group allied to the Classic Maya" (1941:16). Edward Weyer, after a short visit with the northern Pethá group, speculated that his Lacandon "friends" may have helped build the Temple of Inscriptions at Palenque, and that they had lived isolated from other Lacandon groups since the Chol *reducciónes* of 1695 (1957:319). James Nations and Ron Nigh discussed the preservation of "traditional" subsistence strategies in a 1980 article on tropical rainforest agriculture. Robert Bruce and Victor Perera argued that the Lacandon were the descendants of the nobility who ruled the Classic Period Maya site of Palenque in their 1982 book *The Last Lords of Palenque*. In my book *Life, Ritual, and Religion among the Lacandon Maya* (1990), I went on at length about "traditional" Lacandon religion. And in a recent Lacandon ethnography, Boremanse (1988) discusses "traditional" aspects of Lacandon life in his book *Hach Winik*.

However, in order to establish what are in fact traditional behaviors, that is, ones that have persisted over long periods of time, it is necessary to have a detailed knowledge of Lacandon history. In other words, to legitimately discuss the traditional aspects of Lacandon religion, agriculture, and social structure, it is first necessary to know how Lacandon men and women acted out those activities in the past. Unfortunately, there is very little concrete information about Lacandon society before Tozzer's work in the early 1900s, and a great deal of his work is either unknown to the general public or inaccessible. Consequently, speculation about traditional Lacandon activities is largely an act of ethnographic imagination. They are traditional only because authors have labeled them so. In light of this state of affairs, a good place to begin a discussion of change in Lacandon society is to establish what we know about them from earlier work.

## Lacandon Life from 1790 to 1903

There is no direct evidence of what life was like for the ancestors of the contemporary Lacandon before the 1790s and the founding of the San José mission south of Palenque. What Father Calderón and others reported in their letters is that the men of San José were farmers who grew a wide variety of crops, although the crops they cultivated were not specified. Lacandon men practiced polygyny and were not Christian according to these sources. It was also observed that Lacandon men prayed and made offerings to gods who were worshipped in a ceremonial structure separate from the community. They traded forest products for metal tools, cloth, salt, and other manufactured items. Observers commented that men and women both wore a long one-piece cotton tunic, men had shoulder-length hair, and women wore multiple strands of glass bead necklaces acquired through trade with the people of Palenque. Very little is said about women in these reports. If we extrapolate back from nineteenth-century observations they presumably processed the products of the *milpa*, wove cotton cloth, and supervised the care of children.

After a gap of almost one hundred years, the Lacandon again appear in the accounts of late-nineteenth-century travelers and explorers like Charnay, Sapper, and Maler. The best ethnographic information on turn-of-the-century Lacandon in the northern zone comes from Alfred Tozzer, who worked among the Lacandon at Lake Pethá in 1903 and 1904. What can be gleaned about the lives of men and women from Tozzer's observations? Let's start with what would have been immediately apparent to someone walking into a Lacandon compound in 1900. First and foremost, the Lacandon were farmers who settled in multifamily hamlets in the middle of their *milpas*. On the edge of these compounds was an open structure with a long, low thatched roof where Lacandon men practiced their rites and stored ceremonial implements such as incense burners and incense boards called *xikals*. In addition to the customary *milpa* farming and rituals, we also know that Lacandon men were actively trading bows and arrows, produce, and tobacco with workers in the *monterías*. Alternatively, men traveled to nearby towns to sell these items in order to buy goods such as metal tools, salt, sugar, and coffee. Walking through the hamlet you would have seen a few store-bought items such as machetes and axes, some pieces of china, a mirror, bolts of cloth, maybe a nineteenth-century musket, and necklaces of glass beads. However, the majority of people's tools and utensils were manufactured from the materials in their *milpas* and the forest. Palm thatch was used for roofing the dirt-floored shelters. People ate and stored food in gourd bowls, plates, and woven net bags called *ba?ay*. Women ground corn by hand with stone *manos* and metates, and men hunted with finely crafted bows and arrows. By all accounts, Lacandon men and women were still wearing the *xikul* (tunic). Men wore their hair long and uncut about their shoulders, women are described as wearing their hair in one long braid with bird feathers as decoration.

## Men's and Women's Work

Given the volume of tasks necessary to maintain a household in a subsistence-level society it is not surprising that the Lacandon lived in multifamily compounds. From Tozzer's letters and reports it is clear that men and women depended on each other for specific kinds of work. He wrote, "The father, assisted by his oldest son, clears the forest to make the fields and carries on the rites of their religion, while the mother and the daughters spin and weave the cotton into clothing, grind the corn, and carry on the ordinary work of the household" (1978:45). Even though Tozzer did not focus his attention on women's work, from his comments in passing we know that women were occupied with a wide variety of tasks. Tozzer mentioned women helping their husbands clear *milpas* for planting, cutting firewood, weaving baskets and net bags, making agave fiber cord with which they knotted hammocks, and stringing and wearing multiple necklaces made from the seed of plants called *chancahla* and *säkpähen* (Job's tears). He noted that women were grinding corn with stone metates and making tortillas, *posole,* and tamales, and observed that the greater part of a woman's day was taken up with preparing corn for meals.

Tozzer also mentioned that women spun and wove cotton thread and he photographed a woman working with a back strap loom. However, he observed men and women wearing the standard *xikuls* made from manufactured cloth and he feared the knowledge of weaving would die out because of the availability of machine-made cloth (1978:55). With corn preparation required for meals on a daily basis, grinding corn and making tortillas must have been virtually universal among Lacandon women. At the same time, because Lacandon were purchasing manufactured cloth with money from the sale of bows and arrows and tobacco it is reasonable to assume that not all women had to spin and weave. I think it most likely that each household had a woman or two who was familiar with weaving while all woman assisted in preparing corn.

Although Tozzer did not write about the care of children in the Lacandon hamlet where he camped, he mentioned them hanging around his hut at meal times, and he observed that women typically carried infants in net bags on their backs when going about their daily business. From this we can infer that the care of children was the responsibility of women and their older daughters.

From Tozzer's perspective the primary responsibility of Lacandon men was making *milpa* and overseeing the spiritual and physical well-being of their families. Men's days were spent clearing and working in their *milpas* and conducting religious rites, which Tozzer believed were primarily concerned with their fields and the health of their families. Tozzer wrote that between hills of corn Lacandon farmers planted black beans (*buul*) and sweet potatoes (*is*) and he listed a variety of crops in the *milpas* that surrounded his compound (see Table 2.1).

Because he was primarily interested in religion, Tozzer did not specifically study Lacandon agriculture, so we have little direct information about the farming techniques of the turn-of-the-century Lacandon. However, Lacandon farming techniques were studied extensively by Nations and Nigh in the 1970s, before the widespread advent of roads, electricity, and large-scale orientation to tourism. Thus it is reasonable to assume that the practices described by Nations and Nigh, and which I have observed among elderly Lacandon, resemble those of the previous generation studied by Tozzer.

Tozzer was impressed with the quality of Lacandon hunting bows, and he considered hunting to be the second most important activity in which men engaged, after cultivating corn (1978:53).

**TABLE 2.1    Crops in a Turn-of-the-Century Lacandon *Milpa***

| | | |
|---|---|---|
| Achiote | Cotton | Manioc |
| Aguacate | Gourds | Oranges |
| Anona | Grapefruit | Papaya |
| Bananas | Guanabana | Pineapple |
| Black Beans | Guayaba | Sugarcane |
| Cacao | Lima Beans | Sweet Potatoes |
| Chayote | Limes | Tamarindo |
| Cherry Tomatoes | Maize | Tobacco |
| Chicosapote | Mamey | |
| Chilis | Mango | |

*Source:* Adapted from *A Comparative Study of the Mayas and Lacondones* by Alfred M. Tozzer, 1978 (1907), New York: AMS Press, pp. 21–23.

He listed deer, turkeys, wild boar, partridge, armadillo, quail, howler monkeys, spider monkeys, and agouti as the most common forms of game. He also described men fishing and listed turtles, turtle eggs, freshwater crabs, and snails as additional sources of protein.

There is another aspect of hunting that Tozzer did not mention which must have been important. Lacandon men today commonly hunt in abandoned *milpas*. Because there is a greater concentration of food sources in a *milpa* than the surrounding jungle, once a *milpa* is no longer actively occupied animals start sneaking in to forage. Turn-of-the-century *milpas* must have attracted game animals as they do today.

Despite Tozzer's preoccupation with hunting, and although I am sure the Lacandon took full advantage of the variety of game in the forest and abandoned *milpas*, there may not have been much meat on turn-of-the-century Lacandon tables. In his letters Tozzer mentioned eating only turtles and turtle eggs, freshwater snails, fish, monkey (typically used as a filling for ceremonial tamales called *nahwah*), and partridge. Most of the meat he ate in the compound was beef he bought from the *monterías*. Although he spoke of acquiring eggs, he never mentioned any chickens running around the compound where he stayed.

Lacandon men also spent considerable time in ritual activity. Praying and burning incense offerings were daily activities geared toward preserving the well-being of the *milpa* and curing the ailments of family members. Tozzer was lucky to observe an incense burner renewal ceremony because these took several weeks to prepare and carry out. In terms of the amount of time spent, it is clear that Lacandon men's days were filled primarily by *milpa* work and religious obligations. Tozzer also mentioned beekeeping and pottery making in the compound but did not say whether men or women engaged in these activities. Because honey was used to make the ceremonial drink *balché* it is a good bet that men tended the bees. Similarly, if Tozzer observed the making of pottery in any detail he was probably watching men work. However, because he mentions pottery making only in passing it may indicate that this was primarily women's work and he did not pay close attention to it. Tozzer knew enough about Maya gender roles to know that an unrelated man following women around and openly watching them was a serious violation of accepted behavior and would have been interpreted as an indication of sexual interest that would have jeopardized his place in the compound.

## Religion

Until the mid-1990s the essential elements of Lacandon ritual remained largely unchanged for several hundred years. Comparing Tozzer's observations and my own work in the 1980s to the descriptions of Lacandon rituals from San José in the 1790s, it is clear that many of the fundamental elements of Lacandon ritual practice such as god pots, copal incense, *balché*, and bark cloth headbands have remained the same.

Lacandon religious ceremonies typically revolved around the offering of incense and food stuffs to deities through the *läkil k'uh*, or god pots, incense burners dedicated to each god (see Figure 2.1). God pots were conceptualized as living beings who were ensouled in the month-long incense burner renewal rites. The incense burners were the focus of Lacandon ritual activity because they were the medium for communicating with the gods, and the vehicle for transmitting offerings. Lacandon men told me that during a ritual, gods descend to the god house, partake of their

**FIGURE 2.1**   Lacandon god pot.

offerings and drink their *balché* when it is placed on the out-thrust lip of their god pot.

For years I thought that the incense burners were only a physical replica of the god to whom they were dedicated. I was surprised to discover that the men I interviewed believed that the god pots were alive. When making a god pot, one of the most important elements was a small object that was placed in the bottom of the incense burner's bowl. Tozzer who observed the ceremony at a distance believed the god pot makers placed "idols" in the bowls of the newly made incense burners (1978:140). In fact, stones taken from the site of Yaxchilan were deposited in the bowls. These were the *kanche,* or benches, that the gods sat on when they participated in their rites.

The foodstuffs offered to the gods in the traditional ceremonies were of two types: inedible offerings that were transformed in the ritual process to spiritual food and actual food offerings that were shared among ritual participants (see Table 2.2). In all cases, the food offered to the gods was transformed in the ritual context. The most common type of spiritual food was *pom,* or copal incense. I was told that burning incense fed the gods because the incense was transformed into tortillas. In the early 1980s, men in the house compound in which I lived burned these "tortilla" offerings in their god pots on a daily basis.

Ritualized inebriation was also long a part of Lacandon religious rites. Most ceremonies I attended required drinking large quantities of the fermented mead *balché.* Although most Lacandon men told me they drank *balché* to get drunk, ceremonial lead-

TABLE 2.2    Lacandon Offerings

| Offerings | Symbolic Referent |
| --- | --- |
| *Pom* (copal incense) | Tortillas |
| *K?iik?* (rubber figures) | Servants for the gods |
| *Xikal* (incense board) | Human offerings |
| *Chäk hu?un* (bark headbands) | Blood-soaked cloth |
| *K?uxu* (achiote/annatto) | Human blood |
| *Balché* (mead) | *Balché* |
| *Nahwah* (tamale) | Human flesh |
| *Säk ha?* (atole) | Corn gruel |

ers said that drinking *balché* purified one's spirit and put the gods in a good mood when one had to make a request of them. *Balché* was also supposed to induce the state of consciousness in which one was able to speak directly with the gods.

I participated in dozens of ceremonies that featured *balché*. Most of these rites were thanksgiving ceremonies for good harvests or for curing serious illnesses. Because the well-being of the *milpa* is of crucial importance to most Lacandon, as well as a popular social activity, offering *balché* was a common ritual activity throughout the year. The sponsor of the ceremony brewed *balché* in a *chem*, a dugout canoe made from the hollowed-out trunk of a mahogany tree. *Balché* is brewed by fermenting a mix of water, a sweetener such as honey or sugarcane, and strips of the bark of the *balché* tree (*Lonchocarpus longistylus*). The ingredients are mixed in the *balché chem*, which is covered with palm and banana leaves while the *balché* ferments for two to three days. At daybreak on the appointed day, the men of the compound assembled to make their offerings and drink.

In general, the *balché* ceremony was a daylong affair because the drink was totally consumed and not saved for later consumption. After the gods were fed their *balché*, the men sat down on their seats in the god house to pray and drink. Although it is mildly alcoholic, ritual participants drank such large quantities of *balché* that they became very inebriated and often passed out or had to be carried home at the end of the day. Because I am bigger and heavier than most Lacandon men *balché* does not affect me in quite the same manner. In my case a good dose of *balché* induced a pleasant goofiness, much like the woozy feeling people have after taking an over-the-counter cold or allergy remedy.

As pleasant and social as spending a day drinking *balché* might be, there was an underlying serious purpose for the ritualized drunkenness. *Balché* was not brewed for recreation; it was the means by which men communicated with their gods. You don't play with the vehicle through which you speak to God. In the twenty years in which I participated in rites featuring *balché*, no one I interviewed admitted speaking to the gods. However, most men claimed that the man in whose compound I lived, Chan K'in Viejo, could speak to the gods. Chan K'in Viejo denied this claim saying that his father was the last *to'ohil* to communicate directly with the deities and that his father said the gods' voices sounded like the high-pitched buzzing of bees.

# Marriage and Household Life

Given the tasks required to support a Lacandon household and the division of labor reported by Tozzer it would have been virtually impossible to be single and live by oneself. Marriage seems to have been universally practiced. The only single people reported are children or elderly women whose sons helped support them. Although there are few actual cases cited, most visitors including Tozzer wrote that Lacandon men could have more than one wife and that men often married sisters, a practice referred to as sororal polygyny. However, Tozzer, Maler, and the rest never visited a large sample of Lacandon families, so it is impossible to know how widespread this practice was.

Gertrude Duby-Blom and Franz Blom's descriptions of mid-twentieth-century Lacandon life are probably the most accurate of all the accounts written to that time. Because they traveled widely throughout southeastern Chiapas and repeatedly visited numerous Lacandon *caribales* during the 1940s and 1950s they were familiar with a wide sample of Lacandon families. This allowed them to get a broader picture of Lacandon life than was obtained by earlier visitors.

Although not as isolated as supposed by the Bloms, in many respects, the lives of the Northern and Southern Lacandon that they observed had not changed substantially from the Lacandon of the previous century. Although men were hunting with shotguns by the 1940s, the sale or trade of bows and arrows, tobacco, and other *milpa* produce for manufactured goods was started by the eighteenth-century Lacandon of San José. Women continued to spin cotton thread, which they sewed with steel instead of bone needles, and they still knotted hammocks and wove baskets. Enamel cookware was replacing clay and gourd vessels at this time and households commonly had metal corn mills, but many women still ground their corn by hand using stone metates.

When the Bloms began their visits in the 1940s, the Jatate and Cedro-Lacanha groups still lived in thatched homes without walls, much like the shelters described by visitors in the eighteenth and nineteenth centuries (see Figure 2.2). Groups of related families built their homes together in clearings near their *milpas*, but *caribales* were separated about a day's walk from one another. Despite the separation, the inhabitants of distant compounds reg-

FIGURE 2.2    Lacandon home near Jatate River, photographed by
Gertrude Duby, 1944.

ularly visited one another, traded, and occasionally celebrated
joint religious ceremonies.

The northern group formed a separate territorial unit, and
had limited contact with the Southern Lacandon. The people of
the north, living at a slightly higher altitude, built more substantial homes. Although roofed with palm thatch, structures built by
people of the northern group had walls made of boards or sticks
tied together with vines. Neither group used much furniture
other than hammocks, stools, and a table for grinding corn. Food
was hung from the rafters in gourd bowls or net bags. Most
households kept chickens.

The Bloms thought that the Lacandon they visited were living examples of the past. Indeed, they found many continuities
from the Maya of the eighteenth century to the people they visited. However, many of the changes in Lacandon households that
the Bloms considered to be new were actually the result of
processes started at the end of the eighteenth century. For example, the Lacandon had acquired steel axes, machetes, and knives
for their *milpa* work by the 1800s. Additionally, the Bloms noted
that few women owned looms, and Lacandon wore clothes

largely made from manufactured cotton cloth. This was not a new shift in Lacandon life, as the use of manufactured cloth was noted by Tozzer in 1903.

In addition to the axes, machetes, and cloth acquired by Lacandon families, Franz and Trudy Blom observed some Lacandon men in the southern groups wearing ordinary pants and shirts. Women, they noted, still wore the long tunic over a skirt, but also typically wore multiple strands of glass beads, earrings, and hair combs. The Bloms spoke of these changes as new innovations in the Lacandon society and do not seem to have realized that the Lacandon had been acquiring steel tools and beads and earrings since the 1790s, and that Tozzer and Maler had met Lacandon who worked for the lumber companies and dressed in the style of their Mexican contemporaries. I presume the Lacandon of the San José mission who married into Palenque families in the 1790s also conformed to local Spanish styles.

Comparing the Bloms' observations to earlier accounts it is clear that the overall pattern of work and social relationships in Lacandon society was largely unchanged, despite the technological innovations in the three decades between Tozzer's departure from the Lacandon Jungle and the Bloms' arrival. Fran and Trudy Blom visited communities where men hunted with shotguns and women ground corn with metal hand mills, but men were still hunting and women still grinding corn as they had done in the nineteenth century. The preparation of *milpas* and tending of crops were still regarded as a man's responsibility. Men made bows and arrows and clay pots, built houses and dugout canoes, and conducted religious rituals in the god house as they had in the nineteenth century. Women prepared corn, cooked, fetched water, wove and spun cotton cloth, took care of chickens, and tended children, much as they had done in San José in the 1790s.

As other observers before them, the Bloms also commented on the practice of polygyny in Lacandon settlements. They noted that it was common for men to have two or three wives, and that older married men often took small girls as a second or third wife. The young girl would be raised in the household by the older wives as if she were one of their daughters. She would not be sexually active with her husband until she came of age in her early teens.

The Bloms' observations on Lacandon marriage are also borne out by the life histories I have collected among Lacandon women. I have interviewed several of these child brides who are now elderly widows and they tell similar stories. Common themes in their accounts were being taken from their homes as small girls, missing their mothers, being afraid of their husbands, and resisting the first sexual advances. One woman laughed as she described biting and kicking her husband the first time he approached her for sex. Although the women I spoke to had not had a voice in the choice of a husband, they also laughed when they talked about their marriages and spoke affectionately of their husbands. I will discuss two women's stories in greater detail later.

The Lacandon of the 1930s and 1940s followed the same gender division of labor as their ancestors, that is, men farmed and hunted while women processed the products of the *milpas,* cooked, and watched over children. But other aspects of Lacandon life were changing. Men hunted with firearms and sold bows and arrows to buy flashlights, batteries, and radios. Although most Lacandon continued to wear the *xikul,* weaving was largely out of fashion and some Lacandon wore pants and shirts. The old-style open-sided, thatched roof dwellings were giving way to structures with pole and board walls.

Today, the typical home has a cement slab floor and a tin roof. Most households have television and videocassette recorders; some have satellite programming. Some men make *milpa,* others spend most of their time making crafts to sell to tourists. Women in general still prepare meals, but many women prefer to use an instant tortilla mix, rice, and pasta rather than spend hours grinding corn. One sees *xikuls* alongside pants and shirts; young women generally dress in modern-style dresses and wear makeup.

So what does the term *traditional* mean when talking about the Lacandon? It is easy to identify general patterns of behavior that have persisted since the eighteenth century. For example, Lacandon men have traditionally been defined as the makers of *milpa* and hunters. Women have been generally identified as the people who prepare food, weave, and have supervisory responsibilities over children. Polygyny persists in some isolated Lacandon households. Surprisingly, commerce with townspeople is a traditional behavior much to the surprise of those romantics who do not realize the Lacandon have been trading or selling goods to the people of Palenque since the 1790s.

# The Disappearance of Traditional Religion

Today when visitors to Chiapas talk about the traditional Lacandon culture they are typically referring to the non-Christian religious rituals that were practiced by most Lacandon men until the mid-1950s, and persisted in the community of Nahá until the mid-1990s. Numerous historical accounts of Lacandon religious practices demonstrate that the Lacandon practiced a consistent set of religious rituals for the last two hundred years. Eighteenth-century accounts and those of Maler, Tozzer, and the Bloms all indicate that Lacandon men built their own *yatoch k²uh*, literally "god house," separate from their homes on the edge of their settlements. Ritual implements were stored in the structures and both individual and communal rites were conducted there. In *Life, Ritual, and Religion among the Lacandon Maya* (1990), I provided a detailed description of Lacandon rites and ritual paraphernalia as I found them in the 1980s. Ritual activity was largely oriented to ensuring the survival of crops and health of family members. Men were the spiritual caretakers of their families and women were largely excluded from the activities in the god house. Today, however, the non-Christian rituals exist mainly in the exotic tales of travel agents who guide tours in the Lacandon Jungle.

I have thought a lot about Lacandon religion and why most Lacandon so readily abandoned the beliefs that served them for so many years. I asked a number of men who were active in the god houses of the 1980s why they no longer practice the rites and the answer was invariably *"ma² in k²at"* ("I don't want to"). There was no philosophical answer forthcoming. My own thoughts on the issue have revolved around three questions:

1. Why have the rites that allowed men to communicate with the gods been abandoned?
2. The second question follows the first: Men of the nineteenth century were said to have been able to speak with the gods, but now men cannot. What changes occurred in Lacandon ritual that interrupted this bond between men and the divine?
3. The final question that I wrestle with is, Why have most Lacandon abandoned their traditional beliefs without converting to some other belief system?

The answer to the first question is simple. The rituals that allowed men to communicate with the gods have been abandoned because they no longer work. Men no longer talk with the gods after drinking *balché*. I have deduced a possible answer to this question from observations made by Tozzer in 1903 and 1904. Tozzer observed that as they drank *balché* Lacandon men made offerings of their tobacco and cigars and let their own blood by slitting their earlobes. By the time I sat through my first *balché* ceremonies in 1980 the situation had changed. Bloodletting had been abandoned for at least twenty years and I never saw tobacco laid out in front of the god pots as an offering. Furthermore, although most men and many women smoked, few people were growing their own tobacco in the 1980s. I typically saw men smoking Mexican cigarettes. I suspect that the lines of communication with the gods were broken when bloodletting and native tobaccos were dropped from Lacandon rites.

Anthropologists and ethnobotanists have long known that the native peoples of the Americas made full use of the consciousness-altering chemicals found in the plants that grew around them. I am no expert in this area, but walking around the community of San Marcos, Texas, today I can find datura, peyote, mountain laurel, and morning glory, all of which had ritual use in Native American society. Tobacco too played a major role in many cultures. People in the Americas used tobacco as an analgesic and purifying agent, and to induce altered states of consciousness. Shamans in many societies cultivate special varieties of tobacco and practice nicotine intoxication when performing their spiritual errands (see, for example, Wilbert 1987). Thus reading Tozzer's descriptions of bloodletting and looking at Gertrude Duby Blom's photos of Lacandon in the 1940s smoking huge foot-long cigars, I believe that the combination of *balché,* tobacco, and bloodletting could easily have produced a nicotine/alcohol high and the buzzing sound in the ears that men identified with the voices of the gods. The gods quit speaking when two of the three elements that produced this state of mind were dropped. Unfortunately, I have not tested this theory. Because I neither smoke nor particularly enjoy the taste of *balché,* and prefer to leave my blood inside my body unless it is needed for medical reasons, I am not inclined to conduct a field trial of this theory.

In addition to losing the direct contact with the gods that was experienced by their grandfathers, I think many Lacandon men suffered from a general disillusionment with religion that parallels the increasing time and energy that Lacandon families have invested in tourism. I cannot prove that the shift to a mixed commercial–agricultural economy led to the demise of traditional religion. However, this economic change is associated with several elements that may have contributed to the decline in religious practices.

First, much of Lacandon religion was associated with agriculture, such as ceremonies to ensure good harvests and bring rain for crops. In the last decade, as families experimented with commerce with tourists instead of agriculture, the cycle of agricultural ceremonies lost their purpose and fell into disuse.

Second, as Lacandon households began to generate significant incomes they were able to seek effective medical care in the private clinics in Palenque and San Cristobal. In particular, pregnant women began to seek prenatal care and give birth to their babies in San Cristobal. As Lacandon families began to take advantage of Western medical facilities there was a corresponding decline in the practice of rites for healing and therapeutic incantations. In many societies it has been difficult to provide Western medical intervention because nonindustrial peoples' ideas of sickness and healing are often related to their religious beliefs. The Lacandon, however, did not hesitate to adopt a Western medical view of disease and treatment.

Third, I believe television, brought to the community in the summer of 1993, also contributed to the death of Lacandon religion. This occurred at two levels. First, children now play games based on the cartoon characters they watch on television rather than memorizing the traditional knowledge of the elders. In any society without writing, if the youngest generation does not learn the accumulated wisdom of their elders, then that knowledge is irrevocably lost within one generation. Also, television opened a view of a much larger world than most Lacandon possessed prior to its introduction. Lacandon people knew there was a larger world outside of their jungle. I, for example, came from "across the ocean." But television brought that world into their homes. And this world did not obey the rule of the Lacandon gods. Mythology was inadequate to explain huge cities, modern warfare, global economic trends, and other aspects of the modern industrial world. The Lacandon for the first time had to face the relatively small place in the world that was held by their society and traditional beliefs.

Finally, a primary school was built in Nahá in the summer of 1996, which most boys and girls now attend. Several parents told me they thought knowing how to read, write, and do math were important skills their children needed for the future. They are not necessarily expecting their children to farm *milpa* as adults. The children receive basic literacy and math training in addition to Mexican history, social studies, and other subjects. Thus the mythic worldview that explained the cosmos and the place of humans in it is being replaced by a secular, Western view of the world.

The final question which I cannot answer is why most Lacandon have abandoned their traditional beliefs without converting to some other belief system. At my last count there were half a dozen households of Protestant converts in Nahá, and three households that still maintained god houses. I have seen no other public form of religion practiced in any other household.

## Selling the Traditional Lacandon

Visitors to the *Zona Lacandona* and those who cater to the tourist industry in the area continue to sell Lacandon religion as a point of interest to those who wish to see *traditional* Maya in their native habitat. In San Cristobal and Palenque, tour operators describe the strange ritual practices of the Lacandon in the jungle, omitting the fact that a visitor to the community could also watch CNN or their favorite rerun of *Baywatch*. The people who staff institutions such as Na-Bolom, which organizes projects and tours in the Lacandon communities, typically insist on defining the Lacandon almost exclusively by their religious practices, even though the non-Christian rites have been all but abandoned. In my discussions with Na-Bolom staff I have found it virtually impossible to shake their fixation on religious rituals and ritual paraphernalia as markers of Lacandon identity. Further, this focus on religion, because it was a male activity, means that Lacandon women are excluded from any consideration. My suggestions that Lacandon women might be engaged in interesting activities besides grinding corn have been met with indifference. Apparently the activities of half the Lacandon population are not worthy of consideration when visitors can drink *balché*. The fact is that traditional religious practices are essentially dead. Of the six hundred or so Lacandon, maybe half a dozen households continue to practice the rituals that I arrived in Nahá to study in 1980.

It is worth noting that the Lacandon have participated in the commodification of their religion as well. Men who wear jeans and T-shirts at home don *xikuls* before going to the ruins to set up their tourist displays. One can buy a *baxa k'uh*, a facsimile incense burner, or pay to see Lacandon men make the ritual beverage *balché*.

A few of the households that maintain the traditional rites may even do so strictly for commercial reasons. Although they have god pots, a *balché chem*, and all the outward signs of traditional religion, there is one fundamental difference: Their god houses do not have the proper directional orientation and decorations that their fathers taught me were a necessary preconditions for hosting the gods and they are rarely used unless there are visitors in the community. For some Lacandon men, the rituals they learned from their fathers are now just one more commodity to sell to tourists.

What do Lacandon men think of those who have commodified their heritage in this manner? On the occasions when I have seen younger men paid by tourists to make *balché*, I have asked some of the older men what they think. No one has reacted strongly to this situation. The typical response is something like "That is what he wants to do." And to be fair, it is *their* heritage. They have the right to do what they want with it.

## Two Case Studies and Concluding Thoughts

Let us return now to reexamine the notion of *traditional* Lacandon culture and the notion of the generic Lacandon with which I started this chapter. Historically, we can see that general patterns of behavior have persisted in Lacandon society for several hundred years. However, what does that mean for specific families? Life histories I have collected from elderly men and women in Nahá clearly illustrate that general patterns of behavior that all people describe are models that are not fully adhered to in actual practice. All individuals I have interviewed have lived their lives within the general Lacandon model of behavior in their own unique way. Two cases illustrate this point. My first example is a woman named Koh, who is roughly sixty years old.

In some respects, Koh's life has been very traditional. Koh grew up weaving and grinding corn at her mother's side. Koh also lived in a polygynous household with two other wives. The youngest wife, with whom Koh has a very close relationship, moved into the household when she was about six years old. Koh raised the young girl as if she were her own daughter until the younger woman was old enough to assume adult responsibilities. When I asked Koh about her mother and life as a child, Koh's description of her mother's work exemplified the Lacandons' feminine ideal. She insisted that her mother never went to the *milpa* because that was men's work. Her mother ground corn with a *mano* and metate, prepared meals, and wove and washed clothes for her husband and children. "Women do not make *milpa*," she declared, "that is men's work." However, in virtually the next breath she described how after she married she went with her husband to help him in the *milpa* and that she enjoyed their time working together. Clearing and burning a *milpa* were men's work, she said, but planting and weeding were duties she shared with him. Thus Koh's own experiences support and at the same time contradict the model of women's behavior she describes.

Antonio, a Lacandon elder in his sixties, also talked to me about his mother and father's work. Antonio grew up around Monte Libano in the 1930s. His father made a large *milpa* with a wide variety of crops. However, Antonio said that his father also would help his mother around the house, for example, occasionally grinding corn. In addition to making *milpa*, Antonio's father also earned an income selling bows and arrows and tobacco. What surprised me most about Antonio's story was that he said his father sold lots of bows and arrows so that he could buy a record player (Antonio called it a "Victrolio") and records. He said his father loved to listen to the records and bought them whenever he could.

Antonio also told me about his mother. He said she ground corn for tortillas, and gestured with his hands to show how she made really big tortillas. But she didn't weave he said. She never learned how. She made their clothes but his father bought the cloth. She ground corn, made tortillas, and helped his father plant and weed the *milpa*. According to Antonio, his mother also rolled tobacco that his father sold in the settlement of Capulín.

When thinking about the notion of a *traditional* Lacandon life, there are models of behavior that have remained consistent, for example, men make *milpa* and women grind corn. However, the behavior of individuals has often diverged from these models. The last decade has been a time of tremendous change in Lacandon society and has fueled a cottage industry in reminiscing about the traditional life the Lacandon have lost.

So when we talk about *traditional* Lacandon life what does that mean? In one sense, the answer to this question is that what is traditional about Lacandon life is their continuing adaptation to the changes around them. If there is anything that casts doubt on the notion of the Lacandon as simple, isolated children of the forest, it is the image of Antonio's father at the end of a long day's *milpa* work lighting a cigar, putting up his feet, and winding up the Victrola to listen to music. Those who are in the business of selling the Lacandon to tourists do not discuss selling bows and arrows to buy equipment for household entertainment as a feature of traditional Lacandon life. However, in some households it has been an aspect of life in the jungle for almost four generations. In the 1930s, Antonio's father listened to his records on a wind-up Victrola. Today, Antonio's grandchildren watch a television that was bought with money made from bow and arrow sales. The traditional pattern is that Lacandon men sell things in order to buy items for household entertainment. The only thing that has changed is the entertainment technology that is available.

If the term *traditional* refers to behaviors that have persisted over time, then one of the dominant aspects of traditional Lacandon life is that they have had commercial interactions with people from outside the forest for as far back as we can document their presence in Chiapas. Second, it means that, in general, men hunted and made *milpa*, but that women typically helped them with most of the chores required to produce their crops such as planting, weeding, and harvesting. Women, on occasion, even helped their husbands hunt or hunted on their own out of necessity. Third, *traditional* means that virtually all women ground corn and processed *milpa* products into food they cooked for their families, but that men sometimes helped around the kitchen too.

Fourth, it means that some women wove cotton cloth on a back strap loom but others did not, preferring to sew clothes with manufactured cloth.

In other words, the traditional life of the Lacandon was the work men and women shared to support their households and raise their children. Women regularly did what was defined as "men's work" and men occasionally performed what the Lacandon define as "women's work" when it was required. The cases of Koh and Antonio illustrate that Lacandon tradition is not a monolithic concept that can be universally applied to all families. Instead it is a general set of expectations that people have tended to follow in their own unique ways, in order to meet the challenges that life in the Lacandon Jungle presented to them.

# CHAPTER

# 3 Watching Life in a Lacandon Community

In Chapter 2, I discussed the notion of traditional Lacandon culture and offered the opinion that the traditional Lacandon do not exist. Rather than finding a uniform pattern of behavior to which all Lacandon submit, I observed that people conform to stereotypical models of behavior to greater or lesser degrees, but no one person exactly fits the model. In fact, to a large degree the traditional Lacandon are a literary creation of authors who have written about them and tour operators who sell an image of the Lacandon that is attractive to tourists.

In order to write accurately about Lacandon lives it is necessary to understand the elements that determine what men and women do. At the most fundamental level, the factors that influence people's roles in Lacandon society are whether they are male or female, single or married, and young or old. Men and women, children and adults, all lead different lives. So Lacandon behavior cannot be accurately discussed in generic terms. Instead there are the behaviors of young single men, middle-aged married men, elderly married men, young single women, middle-aged married women, elderly married women, widows, boys, and girls. The difficulty of describing Lacandon behavior is compounded by the fact that these categories are not static. Over time, people move in and out of them. Children I met in 1980 are now adults with their own children to care for and married couples have been separated by death. So some observation that might have been common among a category of people in 1980 may no longer be valid. General statements I could make about a Lacandon family in 1980 are very different from what might be true today for that couple's children who have abandoned *milpa* farming for tourism-related work.

I have watched events in the lives of three generations of a single family. In the summer of 1980, I moved into the house compound of a Lacandon elder named Chan K'in Viejo. At that moment in time, Chan K'in Viejo had three wives, five children living with him, and seven married sons and daughters living nearby. He fathered an additional five children before his death in 1996. Today, all but his youngest children have children of their own and comprise a group of one hundred people, almost half the population of Nahá. The lives of these men, women, and children are my model for Lacandon lives and it is the members of this family who provide the examples discussed in this chapter. The kin diagram in the appendix depicts the relationships of the families and individuals discussed in this and the next chapter.

In opening this chapter, I stated that there was no monolithic Lacandon behavior. However, people do not act randomly. They follow patterns of behavior that are, generally speaking, regular and acceptable within certain ranges. In Lacandon society one's range of suitable behavior is primarily determined by sex. Being male or female establishes the boundaries of behavior at the most general level. The degree to which a family participates in the tourist trade is also a factor that significantly affects how a Lacandon household is run, and this has changed long-established Lacandon gender roles during the last two decades. However, tourism is the principal subject of Chapter 4 so I will defer a discussion of men, women, and the tourist industry for the time being. In this chapter I will confine my discussion to families whose main economic efforts are directed to *milpa* farming.

## An Overview of Women, Men, and Work

In general, Maya men and women in *milpa*-based farming families have specifically defined gender-based activities that have been well documented since the sixteenth century (Clendinnen 1982). Farm labor is family labor for Lacandon families without the means to hire others to work for them, and rights to labor were traditionally assigned by gender and marriage. In Lacandon society this gendered pattern of labor resulted in men's and women's activities being separate but interdependent and complementary. For example, making *milpa* is defined as men's work in Lacandon society. A woman's role is to process the products of those *milpas*. Thus in turn-of-the century *milpas* some men cultivated cotton, and women, using their specialized skills in spinning and weaving, transformed the cotton into garments for the members of their families. Before the advent of large-scale tourism, a boy became a man and was eligible to marry when he made his own *milpa* and proved he could support a family. Correspondingly, most women grew up working at their mother's side learning to grind and cook corn, spin thread and weave, and care for children. Each set of activities complemented one another and provided for the household's support.

## Men's Work

In the 1980s, the primary activity of most men of all ages was cultivating their *milpas* and conducting the religious rites that protected their families and fields. Today, the religion I studied in the 1980s is largely gone and some households support themselves through tourism-related activities. Although few families support themselves solely through making *milpa*, *milpa* work in the farming families remains much the same as it was at the turn of the century. *Milpa* work primarily involves clearing plant growth from a selected site, burning the dry underbrush in the field, and almost immediately thereafter planting. Because men work *milpas* in different stages of production and cultivate twenty to thirty different crops, agricultural activity is a year-round effort. Similarly, before the non-Christian religion was abandoned in the 1990s, religious activities were a daily responsibility of Lacandon men. Unlike women, however, men do not work all day, every day. *Milpa* work can be arduous, but the *milpa* does not require daily attention. Furthermore, *milpa* work generally begins early and ends by late morning as the temperature rises.

Another resource of which Lacandon men take advantage is the *pak che kol*, or fallow *milpa*. While *pak che kol* are not actively cultivated, Lacandon farmers do not abandon them. Fruit trees are planted in deserted *milpas* and farmers continue to harvest leftover plant crops and species of wild plants from them. Furthermore,

Lacandon farmers in a sense manage their abandoned *milpas* by encouraging the growth of certain wild plants. Consequently, regeneration of the soil occurs more quickly than that in the *milpas* of other Maya groups (Ron Nigh 1996: personal communication).

Once it is no longer actively occupied by human beings, the fallow *milpa* also attracts game animals. Lacandon men hunt wild game to supplement their crops. Planned hunts are rare. Typically, men hunt opportunistically; that is, they carry their rifles with them to the *milpa* and watch for game. Even boys begin to hunt for small game, such as birds, as soon as they are old enough to use a slingshot.

Religious responsibilities such as those described in Chapters 2 and 5 were exclusively the duty of men in Lacandon society, and boys learned how to make the sacred beverage *balché*, pray, and conduct the rites working at their father's side. In addition to their prayers and daily offerings of incense, men had to gather copal resin for the incense, make ritual implements such as bark-cloth headbands and *balché* drinking gourds, and maintain their family's god house and incense burners. Making god pots was the most arduous of rites as it required a month to six weeks of full-time effort, during which men secluded themselves and slept in the god house. Because the incense burner renewal rite was until recently a yearly event, the ceremony required a huge investment of a man's time and energy.

Although women had no ritual responsibilities in the god house their domestic activities also extended into religious life. It was women who made the food offerings fed to the gods in Lacandon ceremonies. Further, rites such as the incense burner renewal ceremony required the extended effort of women who had to support their husband's and father's efforts by preparing large quantities of ritual foodstuffs as well as feeding the men sequestered in the god house.

## Women's Work

In Lacandon families whose primary subsistence activity is farming, women and girls of all ages typically spend their days on household-based tasks, in particular, food processing and the care of children. As in most Maya societies, a woman's customary tasks involve work that is conducted around the home, and her primary working space is the kitchen.

A Lacandon woman's day begins at sunrise when she grinds corn for her family's morning tortillas. The processing of corn for tortillas and preparation of other staple foods such as beans and corn gruel is a never-ending chore. It is the most time-consuming of all their tasks and absorbs most of the day. Additionally, women spend long hours scrubbing laundry by hand in nearby streams. Completing a load of laundry from wetting it down to folding the sun-dried clothes also takes most of a day. In between these major tasks, women weave baskets, prepare gourds for utensils, and make other household implements. They also haul water, gather firewood, work in their gardens, and raise chickens. Although I was entirely focused on men's activities during my first years in Nahá, the soft rhythm of hands shaping tortillas and the pistol shot–like crack of cloth beaten on rocks in a stream were ever-present sounds that formed the background of my days in the Lacandon Jungle.

Lacandon women in farming households work all day, rarely stopping to rest. In addition to their household tasks, women and children also perform certain types of *milpa* work, such as weeding, and harvesting, and most women in Nahá plant small house gardens where they grow various plants, herbs, vegetables, and flowers. As Tozzer observed, they also grow plants for the colorful seeds which they string together to make necklaces. About the only thing that women do not do anymore is weave. From the descriptions provided by Maler, Tozzer, and others, it appears that weaving was already in decline by the early 1900s as manufactured cloth became available for purchase. Today, only a few women in Nahá still claim to know how to weave, and to my knowledge no women do so.

As previously described, Lacandon gender roles have traditionally been defined by the production and processing of food, principally corn. Lacandon men were defined by their ability to make *milpa*. Correspondingly, Lacandon women were defined by the processing of food produced in their husband's, father's, or son's *milpa*. Thus the tasks a woman performed were delineated by the productive activities and ages of the men in her life. Similarly, the work of widows is directed by the absence of men in their lives.

Widows in Nahá have a special status. A woman's husband is responsible for providing food for the household either by purchase or production in his *milpa*. In previous generations, Lacandon widows would have been supported by their closest male relatives, but this is no longer the case. Because their brothers and sons rarely help them, Lacandon widows must now produce as well as process their own food. The extra time consumed in food production added to labor-intensive food preparation, allows Lacandon widows little or no spare time. To help support themselves widows in Nahá typically sell traditional items such as baskets, necklaces, and net bags that they already make for their own use. I have also met two women who cash crop. One grows tobacco to sell to visitors; the other, black beans.

## Family Examples

Chan K'in Viejo and his family exemplify all the issues discussed in this chapter. In the 1980s, Chan K'in Viejo was the head of a very traditional household. If you ignored the battery-powered radio, metal cooking pots, and corn grinder bolted to a table in the kitchen, you would have seen a household very similar to that which Tozzer and Maler described at the beginning of the twentieth century. Chan K'in Viejo, his three wives, and the children still in his household wore the traditional *xikul*. His wives and daughters braided their hair and adorned it with parrot feathers, much like the women described by visitors to turn-of-the-century Lacandon camps. Chan K'in Viejo's household was not Christian. He maintained a god house that he shared with his lifelong friend, Matejo Viejo. This god house was the center of ritual activity for all of the men in the extended family and their sons-in-law. Most of what I learned of Lacandon religion and mythology was taught to me in this god house by the men of Chan K'in Viejo's house compound.

At this time, Chan K'in Viejo had three surviving wives, Koh II, Koh III, and Koh IV. Koh I had died from a snakebite many years earlier. Koh II was the eldest wife; Koh III was the leader of the household and treated Koh IV, the only women in the household with small children (and pregnant when I first arrived) as a younger sister.

Chan K'in Viejo's family cultivated several large *milpas* that they maintained in various stages of production. Chan K'in Viejo, his wives, unmarried sons, and the occasional son-in-law worked together to support the families in the house compound. I arrived at an anomalous period in this family's history in that Chan K²in Viejo's wives spent much more time in the *milpa* than women in other families. In large part, this was due to Chan K²in Viejo's age and the age of his children. In 1983, all but one of the children of Koh III were married and had started their own households, and most of the children of Chan K²in Viejo's youngest wife, Koh IV, were too young to be of much help. At this time, Chan K²in Viejo was at least in his seventies and could not work as hard as younger men. Without older sons or new sons-in-law in bride service, labor was in short supply and all family members were pressed into service in the *milpa*. However, this experience served his wives well; since Chan K²in Viejo's death in December 1996, his two remaining wives (Koh II died in December 1985) have been forced to support themselves and the youngest wife's five remaining children.

The elements of Lacandon life in which I participated in the 1980s were structured largely by the agricultural cycle. To illustrate the patterns I have described, I have reconstructed from my notes a typical day with Chan K²in Viejo and two of his wives, as I observed them in the early eighties.

## Chan K²in Viejo: Summer 1983

Chan K²in Viejo's day typically began around six in the morning with a trip to his god house to burn copal incense in the god pots and recite his morning prayers. Because he shared his god house with Matejo Viejo they often met and discussed the weather, their *milpas*, and local events. I never saw adult Lacandon men go house to house to visit their friends. Children and teenagers hang out at their friends' houses, but adult men do not. For example, Matejo Viejo is Chan K²in Viejo's oldest friend. Matejo's parents died when he was a child (sometime in the 1920s) and Chan K²in Viejo took the starving boy into his household and provided him with food and shelter until he was old enough to support himself. They were close virtually all of Matejo's life. Yet in three years I never saw Matejo in Chan K²in's house or Chan K²in in Matejo's. Adult men meet only in the god house or at the store to discuss community affairs.

Breakfast was usually around seven in the morning when Chan K²in Viejo returned from the god house. Breakfast typically consisted of fresh tortillas, black beans, and leftovers from the previous dinner. Sometimes Chan K'in or his sons drank a gourd bowl of *ma'ats,* a corn gruel that has a slightly bitter taste and fermented corn smell. Most mornings after breakfast the whole family grabbed their machetes and walked out to work in one of their *milpas.* Until the middle of the twentieth century, the Lacandon tended to build their homes in the middle of their *milpas.* This is no longer true, but most families do not travel far to work. Of all the *milpas* I visited none are more than an hour's walk away, most no more than a fifteen- or twenty-minute walk. Chan K'in Viejo's *milpas* were even closer, only about a ten-minute walk from his home.

New *milpas* are cleared when the rainy season tapers off in December and clearing continues through February. Age, arthritis, and an old accident crippled Chan K'in Viejo's hands, so he usually left the work of clearing the fields to his sons and sons-in-law. That year, he paid a Tzeltal Maya named Florentino to clear and burn a new section of *milpa* adjacent to his older field.

Clearing a *milpa* is hard work, but burning a *milpa* is dangerous. The intensity of a *milpa* fire is sobering and I understand the respect with which Chan K'in spoke of a burning *milpa* and the fear that men have of being trapped in a fire. Timing a field's burn is also a gamble. Chan K'in Viejo said that one should burn and plant a field right before the rains come (sometime in May). However, if you burn and plant too soon the seeds get no rain and dry up in the ground. On the other hand, if you wait too long and get caught by the rains your field will be too wet to burn. In either case, your family would face starvation if your relatives did not have enough of a surplus to help you through the year.

While burning a *milpa* is dramatic, the task that actually takes the most time is much more mundane, that is, weeding. After a field is planted with corn, beans, and squash in the spring, the primary task of the summer months is to fight the weeds that threaten to take over a *milpa* before the crops are established. Thus, day after day, Chan K'in Viejo's family was out in the *milpa* by half past eight, pulling weeds, looking at damage caused by insects and animals, wondering about rain, and worrying about the harvest.

During much of these first years, I wandered around the *milpa* trying to be helpful while not causing too much damage. To help me reach that goal, Chan K'in Viejo assigned his son Chan K'in Quinto to follow me around and make sure I did not destroy anything useful. Chan K'in Quinto was about ten years old at this time and was a wonderful source of vocabulary words. Under his direction, I learned to identify a variety of the plants that Chan K²in Viejo's family cultivated.

In general, the family worked until eleven or so in the morning. Then, as the sun got hotter and backs tired, everyone packed up and returned home. The path back to Chan K²in Viejo's compound led down a steep hill and was usually muddy. Negotiating the descent was tricky for everyone, but was always an adventure for me. In the rain and mud I found it impossible to keep socks clean and dry, so like everyone else I wore rubber sandals or boots. However, I was taller and heavier than everyone else in the community and suffered some spectacular falls on the hill—flinging machetes and firewood flying through the air. The family made a game of watching me descend the path waiting to see if I would fall on my butt and slide halfway down. I was just happy to be included in a joke, even if it was at my expense.

Back from the *milpa* Chan K²in Viejo relaxed and waited for lunch. This meal was typically tortillas and beans, although we sometimes had macaroni cooked with tomatoes and I threw in a can of tuna fish now and then. On days when I had no appetite for tortillas, I crisped one over a fire and made *päkbil wah,* or homemade corn chips. Early afternoons were usually downtime for men. Chan K²in Viejo retreated to his house and I was not forward enough to invite myself in. I usually wrote up field notes or napped, listened to the women working in the kitchen next door, and tried to keep busy. When busy, there were few places I would rather be, but rainy days, in particular, were dreary and I missed familiar things—friends and family, and chocolate. I could pick up a broadcast of *Monday Night Football* on my shortwave radio and plugging in an earphone and listening to the game was a little vacation I gave myself.

Chan K²in Viejo usually returned to his god house in the midafternoon and I usually tagged along. He typically spent several hours a day, several days a week, praying and burning incense, particularly if someone was sick. Chan K²in Viejo did not share his family problems with me. At that time, I was not inclined to pry, but it was obvious when children were sick and required his therapeutic incantations and prayers. It was common to see Chan K²in Viejo leaning over a sick child in the god house, praying and touching the child with a rolled palm leaf that has been smoked in incense. Much of Chan K²in Viejo's time was also spent teaching his sons prayers and how to make religious offerings. I photographed Chan K'in Viejo teaching his son K'in how to make the headbands (*hu'un*) out of ficus tree bark, and I spent many afternoons in the god house with him as he made incense boards (*xikals*). I also went with K'in, Chan K'in Quinto, and their younger brother Kayum as they hiked into the hills to gather pine resin for incense.

Dinner was usually around dusk and I was served at the table in the kitchen hut with Chan K'in Viejo and his son K'in. The women rarely sat down to eat. They usually kept busy making tortillas and serving children, and ate on their feet as they worked. Koh II occasionally sat down next to Chan K'in Viejo at the end of a meal and smoked a cigar, but that was so rare that I was surprised when it happened. The younger children sat at a small table next to where the older boys and men sat.

After dinner, while still at the table, I usually interviewed Chan K'in Viejo, taped stories he recited, or asked for his help with my tape transcriptions. He actively encouraged my work because he believed the younger generation was not learning this information, and he commented about how I would write the stories down and preserve them for the future. We usually continued until he ran out of things to say or my brain finally melted down from concentrating so hard to understand the Maya. I usually tired before he did. Then I would excuse myself and head for my hammock. I knew that Chan K'in Viejo stayed up later because I could hear him talking with his wives and listening to the radio in their house next door. However, I was not comfortable inviting myself into his home and I know little of what went on there during my first years in Nahá.

Although the focus of family work in Chan K'in Viejo's compound was the *milpa*, Chan K'in Viejo also derived a secondary income from the tourist trade. As a young man, Chan K'in Viejo would pack bundles of tobacco and bows and arrows on his back and make the three-day hike to the town of Tenosique. There he sold his goods to buy household items such as salt, cloth, and machetes. When he had acquired all the articles he could carry, he would make the three-day walk home. As an elderly man, he no longer sold or traded items directly; instead he helped produce crafts that were sold by his sons and for which they gave him a share of their profits. For example, in October 1981, I watched Chan K'in Viejo and his wives working over a fire drying and

**FIGURE 3.1**   Drying *oh⁷*

straightening long reeds called *oh⁷* that were cut to make arrow shafts (see Figure 3.1).

My early studies among the Lacandon focused on their religion, thus I spent most of my time with Chan K⁷in Viejo and his older sons. Because I was not married, the women in his family treated me extremely formally. I would sometimes catch a glimpse of a woman watching me from behind a half-closed door, or over-hear a child describing my activities to his mother, but Lacandon women only communicated with me through their husbands or fathers. Even if I had been interested in their work during my first years in Nahá, it would have been virtually impossible for me to interview or observe women in the community. One interaction that stands out in my memory typifies this state of affairs. I was finishing dinner at the table with Chan K⁷in Viejo, when Koh III walked up beside me. Looking over me, she asked Chan K⁷in Viejo if I wanted more coffee. Chan K⁷in Viejo looked up from his plate and asked me if I wanted more to drink. I looked at him and said, "Yes." He, in turn, looked up at his wife and said, "Juan would like more coffee." Only then did Koh III fill my cup.

I treated Lacandon women with the same amount of reserve. To avoid any suspicion of impropriety, I only addressed Lacandon women through their husbands or sons and was always care-ful never to be alone with them. The only time I would directly address a woman was in public when offering help, such as of-fering to cut firewood or help carry corn home from the *milpa*. The following description of a Lacandon woman's day is much less personal than my account of a day with Chan K'in Viejo because my relationship with Lacandon women at that time was imper-sonal and the information I had on their activities was gathered from the quick impressions I could jot down in passing as the women's activities flowed around me.

This account focuses on Kohs III and IV. Koh II undoubtedly had led a fascinating life but I always felt she considered me the village idiot and never had time to bother with me. Koh II wasn't one to be trifled with. I once saw her castrate a dog on the spot after it had bitten Chan K'in Viejo. Chan K'in Viejo cared deeply for her, and after her death in December 1985 we had several long con-versations about death and what happened in the afterlife. How-ever, for the most part I ignored women's activities in the 1980s. In the early 1990s, when I woke up to the fact that I had been oblivi-ous to the activities of half the Lacandon population, I turned to the Kohs for a look at what Lacandon women were doing.

The Kohs and their daughters are the source of many of the elements of women's lives that I describe at the end of this chap-ter and in Chapter 4. Today I have a close personal relationship with them. When I arrived in Nahá for an unannounced visit in May of 2001 I found them weeding in a *milpa* and was shocked when the elder Koh hugged me and the younger took me by the hand. This is a display of affection that would have been un-thinkable in the 1980s.

## Kohs III and IV: Summer 1986

Koh III and Koh IV have a very close relationship in large part because Koh III raised her "younger sister." Chan K'in Viejo took Koh IV into his household after her father's death, when she was a small girl of about six. She remembers being afraid of him and missing her mother, who today lives about a thirty-minute walk away (see Box 3.1, The Story of Nuk). Koh IV grew up working at Koh III's side, assisting with the endless household tasks and by helping Koh III with her children, a favor that Koh III has repaid by helping Koh IV with her many children.

BOX   **3.1**

## The Story of Nuk

The taking of child brides was common in Lacandon communities during the twentieth century. Many visitors in Lacandon camps in the first decades of the last century comment on it. Although it is common for Lacandon women to marry in their teens, I suspect the practice of taking prepubescent girls into one's household is an artifact of the calamitous drop in the Lacandon population that occurred at the end of the nineteenth century. Although not common today, one tragic instance of this practice occurred between a Lacandon girl and an American man in 1993.

Nuk was a beautiful little girl, born before Chan K'in Sexto in 1978 or 1979. I didn't have much contact with Nuk. A girl her age was typically kept busy helping her mother around the house. I usually saw her playing with other children, or lugging a younger sibling back and forth to the *milpa* following her mother to work. I don't know that I ever talked to Nuk until July of 1993.

I went to Nahá in the summer of 1993 to try to study the Lacandon's conception of the stars and constellations. When I arrived, I was surprised to find Leo Bruce, the nephew of an American linguist named Robert Bruce. Robert Bruce had worked with the Lacandon since the 1950s, and I had known him since my first forays into the Lacandon Jungle. However, even more surprising, I discovered that Leo had "married" the fifteen-year-old Nuk and was building a substantial house in the community, different from all others in that it was raised about eight feet above the ground. I arrived in Nahá just before Leo's thirtieth birthday and because I was a friend of Robert Bruce, Nuk invited me to Leo's thirtieth birthday party. The party was the only opportunity I had to sit down and talk with Leo. I was curious about Leo's presence in Nahá. I knew he was there to help his uncle make a film on the incense burner renewal ceremony that they hoped to sell. But when I asked him why he was building a house in Nahá when he didn't intend to stay and why he, a thirty-year-old man, had married a fifteen-year-old girl, Leo looked at me and replied contemptuously that he came to Nahá to "get away from people like you." Then he walked away. I don't think I saw him again. He never did answer my question about his marriage to Nuk.

On the morning of August 5, just a week or two after I left Nahá, Nuk was dead and I was notified that Leo had been arrested and was being held for trial in Ocosingo. Nuk's body was taken to Ocosingo for an autopsy, which revealed that her neck was broken. Over the next several months Leo sat in the Ocosingo jail while lawyers took statements from Lacandon from Nahá, Robert Bruce, and a variety of other parties. Robert Bruce maintained his nephew's innocence. The men in Chan K'in Viejo's compound were equally sure that Leo had killed Nuk. They told me they had heard her screaming the night of her death but figured that Leo was drunk and they were fighting. They did not know that anything was wrong until early the next morning when Leo ran to Chan K'in Viejo's house saying Nuk had fallen out of the house and hurt herself. When family members ran to Leo's house they found Nuk dead.

I have no idea what happened that night. Leo was the only witness, and I can only report what Nuk's family told me. The case never came to trial. Leo sat in the Ocosingo jail through the fall of 1993. Then on the morning of January 1, 1994, Zapatista rebels occupied Ocosingo, opened the jail, and freed everyone incarcerated there. Leo Bruce slipped away and made his way back to the United States. I do not know where Leo is now, or whether he is innocent or guilty. But the fact that he never stood trial or explained his role in Nuk's death remains a raw wound in Chan K'in Viejo's family. Were he to return to Nahá I am confident that his life would be threatened.

One final note to this sad tale is that Robert Bruce's defense of his nephew deeply damaged his friendship with Chan K'in Viejo. He was not welcome back in Nahá for several years. However, when Bruce died of cancer in the spring of 1997, one of his last requests was to be buried alongside Chan K'in Viejo, who had died the previous December. I was in Nahá when Bruce's daughter brought his ashes to fulfill his last request. A community meeting was held to discuss the situation, permission was granted, and we buried Bruce's urn next to his lifelong friend in the Lacandon cemetery, about ten yards from Nuk's gravesite.

---

Their day began at sunrise when one of the women rekindled the embers from the previous night's fire and began grinding corn and shaping dough for the morning tortillas. Even in a household with a co-wife to share the burden of work, a woman is still responsible for the care and feeding of her own children.

To prepare tortillas, women must first shell the corn (see Figure 3.2), separating the kernels from the dried corncob. This is a relatively simple and quick process that takes perhaps thirty minutes.

**FIGURE 3.2** Shelling corn.

Next, the kernels are boiled for at least eight hours. The Kohs usually boiled enough corn for two days' tortillas so that the process only needed to be repeated every other day. After the corn kernels are cooked they are drained and left to cool. Once the kernels are cooled they are ground in a *molino,* or hand grinder, into *säkpet,* a thick dough that is kneaded and shaped into a ball. The *säkpet* is then either wrapped and put away for future use or put through the grinder a second time for the next meal's tortillas. If it is close to mealtime the dough is kneaded again, then patted out into large ten- to twelve-inch tortillas and immediately cooked. At any given time during the day the women are involved in some aspect of the tortilla-making process. Although half the process, namely soaking and boiling the corn kernels, can be accomplished without the women's complete attention, grinding, kneading, and cooking dough can take two to three hours for each meal because it takes many tortillas to feed a group of hungry children and a husband. Fortunately, the nature of tortilla making is compatible with other necessary household chores.

In addition to the food preparation, the two Kohs were also responsible for the family chickens and turkeys, laundering clothes, and child care. Koh IV had seven children. Two of these children were girls, one of whom was old enough to offer some assistance with the daily domestic chores. Chan Nuk, the eldest daughter typically did laundry, for example. Although sons are capable of performing domestic tasks, the Lacandon have traditionally designated domestic chores as "women's work" and in this household, men did virtually no domestic labor. At one point I asked Koh III to let me grind corn for her, and she suspiciously relinquished control of the *molino's* handle only at her husband's urging. After grinding a few minutes I asked her if she would teach me how to make tortillas but that was too much for her. She emphatically refused, and replied that if I married she would show my wife.

In addition to their child-care and domestic responsibilities, the Kohs helped Chan K'in Viejo and Koh IV's older sons with planting and weeding in the *milpas*. Although the sons generally chopped firewood, it was not unusual to see the women shoulder an armload of wood on the way home.

After the evening meal, the Kohs cleaned the kitchen and either sat down to listen to Chan K'in Viejo's story of the evening, or retired to the main house next door. There they listened to music with Chan K'in Viejo, shelled corn, wove carrying baskets called *xak*, or performed other similar small tasks by the light of a kerosene lamp made from a tin can. Lights were typically out by about ten.

## Childbirth and Infant Mortality

My own marriage in 1994 helped me become more aware of the lives of the women in Nahá. Looking back today, I am embarrassed that I could have lived among these women for so many years and not recognize the importance of their work. I have tried to incorporate data on women's activities in my work since 1995. In fact, I have engaged in a constant battle with individuals and organizations who ask for my help with their Lacandon projects, trying to get them to recognize that Lacandon women's activities are just as significant as men's.

For example, a few years ago staff at the Asociación Cultural Na-Bolom in San Cristobal asked me to consult with them on a project to preserve Lacandon culture. I first asked them what it was they wanted to preserve. Their answer was they wanted to preserve traditional religious practices. As I have discussed earlier, religious rituals are exclusively the province of men. I asked whether they had thought about somehow documenting and preserving a corresponding traditional women's activity, such as spinning and weaving. After all, no spinning and weaving means no clothes—and it gets cold in the Lacandon Jungle in January. There was a moment of silence, and then the project leader said, "Yes, yes but how do you think we can get them to preserve traditional religious practices?" Thus ended the discussion of women's activities.

I first took my wife, Stacie, with me to Nahá in the summer of 1996 when she was seven months pregnant with our first child. By the time we arrived in Nahá, Stacie was worn out by the arduous trip and nauseated by the heat and truck exhaust. The Kohs took over. I was touched by a level of concern and caring that as a single man I had never seen. My wife's presence and condition changed my status in Nahá. At the age of forty-one I became an adult man in the eyes of the people in the house compound. More importantly, my wife's pregnancy opened a window on a set of hopes and fears about sex, pregnancy, and birth shared by women the world over but that, as a man, I had never had to confront. I worried about my wife's health throughout her pregnancies but never had to face any danger during her deliveries. The dangers of childbirth are borne only by mothers and their babies and we all owe our existence to the fact that women are willing to take that risk. Thus I developed a newfound sense of respect for Lacandon women, and for the first time women in Nahá freely discussed topics like birth and menstruation with Stacie and me. They would never have discussed these things with me alone. I had watched women grind corn and pull weeds in a *milpa,* but by accident my wife opened a window through which I could look into Lacandon women's personal lives. And what I learned had more of an emotional impact on me in a few weeks than years of studying religion with Chan K'in Viejo.

Lacandon women refer to the state of pregnancy as *ma'uts,* or "not well," which may refer to the discomfort of being pregnant as they use the same term for menstruation. Women typically asked Stacie if she could feel the baby moving, if she hoped for a boy or a girl, and if she would nurse her baby. They also counseled her not to have sexual relations with me for a month after the baby's birth.

Several women also discussed how painful their deliveries had been and asked if Stacie was afraid. They were surprised that Stacie, who was utterly fearless during her pregnancies and deliveries, was not at all worried. I was the one who worried. I had never thought much about bearing children in the Lacandon Jungle until my wife was pregnant. Even with all the medical care available to us, I worried about my wife's health and the safe delivery of our children. In restrospect, I see that Stacie bore our children in a medically supervised setting with extensive prenatal care, most of which is not available to young Lacandon women because of lack of facilities or the cost. Looking at infant mortality in Nahá I understand why some of the women we talked to were so fearful for their babies. This concern jarred me into a realization of another aspect of women's lives in Nahá that I had never thought about: the dangers of pregnancy and childbirth. It was then that I first considered the effects of the devastating emotional pain of high infant mortality in a society with little pre- or postnatal care. I did not realize the magnitude of these losses until I started reviewing kinship notes I had made of Chan K?in Viejo's family history from 1980 to 1999. I discovered that most of Chan K?in Viejo's children had babies die in infancy or lost young women to complications associated with childbirth.

Before 1999, I had never thought to go through my accumulated field notes to construct a history of Chan K?in Viejo's family. It was far more difficult than I had anticipated. I discovered that over the years I had recorded numerous births that I did not find in kin charts made in subsequent years. At first I assumed that I had made mistakes in my charts, but as the instances of missing babies mounted I realized I had recorded the births of children who had not survived long enough to be named and thus were not being reported by parents when I charted their families.

After meeting my wife, Lacandon women told me that it was bad luck for a pregnant women to discuss her pregnancy, even dangerous for the unborn child. In fact, the Lacandon I know do not celebrate the birth of children or even announce that they have been born. Because Lacandon women do not discuss their pregnancies or announce their births it is difficult to know exactly how many babies die late term or soon after birth. They are never acknowledged as having existed and thus are not reported in family histories. However, children who are old enough to be socially recognized are remembered, and the kin chart reveals a sad picture. These families have suffered the loss of several small children. If you refer to the Kin chart in the appendix you will see that Koh III (#4 on the chart) lost one daughter and grandchild in childbirth. Chan Nuk (#6), the eldest daughter of Koh II lost two daughters in infancy. I recorded the birth of a son to Chan K'in (#8) who died in his first year. The young daughter of K'in (#9), one of Chan K'in Viejo's eldest sons, died in infancy. The first two babies of Nuk (#11), the eldest daughter of Koh III, died as infants, and one of Koh III's younger daughters Chan Nuk (#15) lost a son in early childhood. Kayum (#14), son of Koh III, lost a toddler-age son, and one of Koh's youngest sons Chan K'in Quatro (#17) lost a young son.

The infant mortality rate is in part the basis for the custom of calling a baby *och*, "possum," until it is at least several months old. When a new baby is brought into a household the older children are told it is a possum that was found in the forest and that if it is held enough it will become a human. Dan Renshaw, a teacher in San Antonio who married a woman from Nahá, told me that his wife did not tell her mother she was pregnant and did not reveal the birth of their daughters until they visited Nahá during their summer vacation! I can only imagine how devastating the loss of a child must be. It is mind-numbing to think about the Kohs' experiencing the loss of three of their children, and eleven grandchildren, and it gives me a new appreciation for the lives of women in the community. It also makes the general perception that Lacandon culture is composed only of men's activities even more appalling.

I have now completed a picture of what everyday life was like for men and women in the 1980s before tourism became an alternative to farming. In the next chapter I will describe the economic and political changes in Chiapas that drove the shift from *milpa* farming to tourism in Nahá, and discuss how tourism has changed life in the communities of Nahá and Lacanha.

# CHAPTER

# 4 Three Decades of Change: 1970–2000

Chapter 3 discussed the general pattern of the traditional Lacandon life, and how one's age, marital status, and gender influence the roles that are open to an adult. In this chapter, I would like to discuss how Lacandon lives have changed in response to the Mexican oil economy in the 1970s and the rise of the tourist industry in Chiapas in the 1980s. These factors have had an impact on virtually all aspects of Lacandon life, from agriculture to gender roles to religion. In 1980, I looked at Lacandon life as if it existed in a vacuum. Today, as I learn more about the history of Chiapas, I see that the lives of the Lacandon are intimately tied up with political and economic issues that kept Chiapas in turmoil for most of the twentieth century. The Lacandon had little to do with the political events in Chiapas and were only marginal participants in the state and federal economies. *Milpa* farming had always been the dominant subsistence activity even though Lacandon families sold forest products and produce from their fields to supplement their family incomes and acquire manufactured goods for their households such as machetes, pots and pans, and cloth. However, decisions made in Mexico City and the state capital of Tuxtla transformed their lives. The major change is that, since about 1980, many Lacandon families have shifted increasing amounts of time and energy away from farming to sell handicrafts to tourists in Palenque and San Cristobal.

The Lacandon present an interesting case study of what happens to a culture based on subsistence agriculture that makes a rapid and voluntary transition to a mixed economy based on agriculture and commerce. In terms of profit, this economic shift has been immensely successful for some families. However, surveys of the crops cultivated in Lacandon *milpas* conducted through the spring and summers of 1995, 1997, and 1999, together with economic analyses of several Lacandon households, clearly demonstrate that economic success in selling arts and crafts to tourists has led to a variety of changes in Lacandon material life and social relations. While the Lacandon have been trading with people in Palenque for almost three hundred years, tourism has had a dramatic effect on Lacandon society. In particular, long-established agricultural traditions and their related gender roles have shifted as families have altered their economic strategy from subsistence agriculture to a mixed economy that includes the mass production of bow and arrow sets, clay and wooden figures, and *baxa kʔuh* or "play incense burners," that the Lacandon sell to tourists outside the ruins of the Classic Period Maya ruins of Palenque.

I have divided this chapter into two sections. The first briefly discusses the government policies that encouraged immigration into the Lacandon Jungle, the Mexican oil economy of the 1970s, and the rise of tourism in Chiapas in the 1980s. It goes on to examine how some Lacandon families have taken advantage of the opportunities presented by tourism and how this has affected traditional agricultural practices in the Lacandon communities of Nahá and Lacanha. The second half of the chapter deals with some of the social consequences of tourism in everyday Lacandon life and presents the case studies of two young Lacandon men who grew up during this period.

## Government, Oil, and Immigration: An Overview

Colonization of the Lacandon Jungle by Maya from the highlands of Chiapas has been encouraged by the Mexican government since the 1930s as one mechanism to avoid extensive land reform in Chiapas. In 1940, over half of the farm land of Chiapas was held by only 2.6 percent of all landowners (O'Brien 1998:110). Rather than expropriate land held by wealthy ranchers or farmers, the Mexican government has historically found it easier to encourage land-seeking peasants to colonize the relatively empty forest lands of southeastern Chiapas. The government's distribution of land in the *Selva Lacandona* reached a record pace in the 1970s and 1980s. Nahá is in the *municipio* of Ocosingo. During the 1970s, 171,230 hectares (one hectare is equivalent to 10,000 square meters, or about two and a half acres) of forest land was distributed in the *municipio,* and Ocosingo continued to be the leading *municipio* for land distributions in the 1980s. By 1984, the land distributed in the *Zona Lacandona* exceeded 1 million hectares, including the 614,321 hectares granted to the Lacandon Maya (O'Brien 1998:117). In 1940, less than 5,000 people lived in the *Selva Lacandona*. By 1980, the population had risen to over 150,000; by 1990, the same area housed almost 300,000 people (O'Brien 1998:112).

To a degree, the Lacandon Maya have been sheltered from the economic and political upheavals that have transformed the landscape of Chiapas in the last few decades. This is not to say that they were isolated or unaware of the larger forces influencing Maya peoples outside of the jungle, but rather that the effect of such forces was much less dramatic than in other parts of Chiapas. Different aspects of the political and economic history of Chiapas have been extensively outlined in other places (in particular, see Cancian 1992; Collier 1994; O'Brien 1998) and do not need to be repeated in this work. However, it is useful to examine changes in Chiapas as a whole, to better understand economic and social events in the principal Lacandon communities in a wider context.

As discussed in Chapter 1, the Lacandon lived in isolated extended family compounds scattered throughout the forest and were relatively isolated until the early part of this century. The history of Maya peoples in other parts of Chiapas followed a much different path. Around the colonial capital of San Cristobal de las Casas for example, Maya Indians had little access to land and were typically laborers or tenant farmers on the lands of wealthy plantation owners since the conquest in the sixteenth century (Collier 1975; Wasserstrom 1983). It was not until the agrarian reforms of President Lazaro Cárdenas (1934–1940) that large parcels of land were made available to Indians in the highlands of Chiapas. The Lacandon were distantly aware of the Mexican Revolution that lasted from 1910 to 1921. However, living in the middle of a large expanse of undeveloped forest, these events were of little consequence. Land was plentiful, the influence of the government practically nonexistent, and industrial exploitation of the forest minimal. For a time their lives continued largely undisturbed by outside political events, but by the 1930s and 1940s forces that would have a great impact on them had been set in motion. Encouraged by the passage of agrarian reform laws which opened up unsettled federal lands, new immigrants—Tzeltal and Tzotzil Maya from the highlands of Chiapas—moved down the Ocosingo Valley into the Lacandon Jungle. Tzeltals from Ocosingo, for example, founded the community of Lacandon just a few miles north of Nahá and were given ownership of the land in 1954 (Arizpe et al., 1996:25–26).

Outside pressure on the Lacandon also was exerted from the east as Chol speakers from around Palenque joined the move into the forest. Like the Tzeltal, the Chol immigrants are descended from Indians who were forcibly removed from the jungle in the sixteenth century. Since that time they had toiled as laborers on sugar cane, coffee, and cattle *fincas*. These people received small parcels of land to farm in the reforms of the 1930s; as in the highlands, however, the amount of land was inadequate for the growing population. Families were encouraged to migrate to the forest where they raised corn, coffee, and cattle, as they had when working as debt peons on lowland plantations.

In the 1970s, the agrarian policies of President Luis Echeverría continued to encourage the settlement of Eastern Chiapas. Landless peasants from northern Mexican states, like Sonora and Chihuahua, were given land grants and resettled in the Lacandon forest (Arizpe et al., 1996:28). The current problems with deforestation and erosion in southeastern Chiapas were hastened by this influx of large numbers of people (see Nations and Komer 1982, Rich 1982, and Collier 1994 for more extensive treatments of this topic). However, it is wrong to blame migrating peasants for all the environmental problems in the *Selva Lacandona*. Government policies encouraged colonization of the lands and the production of cash crops for export rather than food crops for domestic consumption.

Even though the Mexican government sponsored the creation of the first forest reserve in 1971, they have at the same time promoted policies that encouraged the area's economic and agricultural development. For example, in May of 1997, the governor of Chiapas announced the investment of more than 122 million pesos in development projects supporting horse and cattle husbandry, increasing of pasture lands, the operation of lumber mills, and fish and bee farming (Chiapas! 1997:11). The consequence of these policies, according to Nations (1984:27), is that in the last fifty years about half the Lacandon forest has been cleared.

Whereas the Lacandon have historically concentrated for the most part on subsistence farming, the farming strategies of the recent Tzeltal, Chol, and Tzotzil colonists have been a mixture of subsistence and semicommercial agriculture. Historically, the primary form of agricultural production in the *Selva Lacandona* was slash and burn. Although surplus corn was always welcome as a potential source of income, the primary goal was to provide food for one's family. However, in the twentieth century the Mexican government encouraged the development and production of commercial crops through subsidized loans and credit for equipment. Today, typical cash crops in the area are coffee, chili, and cacao. Communities in the area around Nahá in particular, produce coffee and chilies for sale and cacao is often intercropped with coffee.

Growing export crops such as chilies may provide a household with badly needed cash, but fluctuations in the market prices of chilies and coffee make it a gamble to invest in these crops. The hazards of cash cropping encouraged many immigrants to the jungle to turn to a more reliable method of producing income—raising cattle. Cattle have had a major impact on land use in the *Selva Lacandona.*

Cattle production in Chiapas increased throughout the twentieth century. Cattle grazing did not become popular in Chiapas until the 1930s when the agrarian reforms of the Cárdenas administration were enacted. At that time, the law allowed large estates dedicated to cattle production to be protected from government expropriation and redistribution. As a result, agricultural lands were increasingly converted to cattle pasture and remained in the hands of the elite (O'Brien 1998:126–127). In addition, after 1950, cattle production became an attractive alternative to crop production because the market for beef was more stable than other commodities and the government provided credits for raising cattle. In 1950, about 480,000 head of cattle were raised in Chiapas; by 1990, this figure had increased to 2,063,000 (O'Brien 1998:126). As the number of cattle increased and the cattle-producing estates expanded, cattle production spread into the the *Selva Lacandona*.

On a smaller scale, cattle raising is attractive to *campesinos* because it can provide a much higher income, faster, than selling surplus corn, chilies, or coffee. A household that farms but also cares for a small number of cattle can sell the cattle for clothes, building materials, maybe even a share of a truck. Cattle are also a means for storing wealth. They can be sold when prices are high or in times of need. Agricultural products, on the other hand, must be sold immediately or they spoil. Cattle also require less labor than agriculture and can supplement a household's farming activities (O'Brien 1998:129). Finally, the government has encouraged cattle production in Chiapas by providing a wide variety of incentives in the form of credits and loans.

Although few Lacandon have tried their hand at cattle husbandry, many in immigrant communities have found cattle an attractive option. By 1990, there were over 150,000 head of cattle in the *Zona Lacandona* (O'Brien 1998:130). Unfortunately, without large tracts of land cattle ranching is productive only in the short term. The small cattle operations run by most immigrant families have overstocked their pastures and overgrazed their lands. If the pasture land is grazed too long, the soil becomes sterile and useless for agriculture or pasture. A drive from Nahá to Palenque, one of the fastest-growing centers of the cattle industry, now shows huge tracts of eroded, burned-out land that supports only the sparsest growth.

The response of many Lacandon families to the pressure posed by immigration and deforestation was to abandon their traditional settlement pattern. Dispersed, extended family compounds, gave way to groups of people congregating in larger communities, such as Lacanha Chan Sayab and Nahá, and led to the formation of the community of Mensäbäk. This change in residence pattern had the political advantage of creating distinct political entities through which appeals for aid could be channeled and recognized.

Rapid economic change between 1970 and 1979 had a major impact on Maya life in Chiapas. Under the administrations of Mexican Presidents Echeverría (1970–1976) and López Portillo (1976–1982) there was a huge influx of federal funds for development in Chiapas. In particular, these funds were channeled into energy development (hydroelectric dam projects), road building, and related construction projects. At this same time, the development of oil fields in the neighboring state of Tabasco brought large amounts of cash into the economy of Chiapas. As these resources became available, the federal government provided a great deal of credit for local development projects in Chiapas. The Socio-economic Development Program for the Highlands of Chiapas (PRODESCH) administered projects in areas such as agriculture, health, and education. However, little of this funding had any visible effect on the lowland areas where the Lacandon lived.

As money poured into the highlands men shifted away from corn farming. They left their home communities to take jobs in construction and the oil fields, and subsistence agriculture gave way to wage labor. Road construction, for example, provided jobs and opened up new opportunities to Zinacantecan Maya who were able to save enough money to purchase trucks and start their own trucking companies. By 1983, corn farming was no longer the dominant occupation among Zinacantecan men (Cancian 1992:25).

The most dramatic change sponsored by the federal government was in 1968 when they formulated plans to create a rain forest preserve in eastern Chiapas to help combat deforestation of the area. Logging by foreign companies had been conducted in the Lacandon Jungle since the early 1800s. But in 1972, a year after the federal government set aside 614,321 hectares of forest for the *Zona Lacandona*, the Weiss Fricker Mahogany Company of Pensacola, Florida, which worked through a Mexican company named *Aserraderos Bonampak*, sold their logging operation to one of the financial organs of the Mexican government, the Nacional Financiera, S.A. (NAFINSA). It was NAFINSA's job to manage the money made logging in the *Selva Lacandona* (O'Brien 1998:76).

The *Compañia Forestal de la Lacandon S.A.* (COFOLASA) was created as the official state-controlled timber operation by presidential decree in 1974 (De Vos 1992:282). COFOLASA contracted with communities in the *Zona Lacandona* for logging rights, and a part of the profits they earned was paid to the Ministry of Agrarian Reform which was to dispense the money in the form of community services (O'Brien 1998:76). Specifically, COFOLASA made the Lacandon in the *Zona Lacandona* gifts of clothes and medicine and promised cash payments for the right to cut timber on their land. However, 70 percent of the timber royalties were placed in a common fund controlled by NAFINSA with the remaining 30 percent distributed among Lacandon heads of families in biannual payments (O'Brien 1998:78).

Most of the mahogany, ceiba, and tropical cedar from the *Zona Lacandona* was logged out by the early 1980s. One logging team foreman reported that in a single period of twenty days his team had cut $2 U.S. million worth of logs (Nations 1984:35). With the proceeds from the lumber contracts, government agencies financed by lumber money distributed by NAFINSA started programs to help the Lacandon "improve" their lives. Lacandon communities received a community truck and were told that a fund had been set up for them in the state capital of Tuxtla. Small stores run by the *Compañia Nacional de Subsistencias Populares* (CONASUPO) that sell items at prices fixed by the state were set up in each community and stocked with cookies, sugar, gum, fruit juices, and ground corn. However, the stores were soon abandoned, taken over by private Lacandon entrepreneurs, and government officials reported that the 7 million peso community fund had been depleted (Nations 1984:36). There was no accounting of where the Lacandon's money had gone.

In addition to the stores and trucks, clinics were built in several of the forest communities, providing access to rudimentary health care when doctors could be found to staff them. In 1979, the first road was bulldozed through to Nahá, connecting the Lacandon community to Palenque in the northeast and Ocosingo to the west.

In 1975, the Zona Lacandona was expanded to 662,000 hectares and ultimately became part of what is now the Montes Azules Biosphere Reserve. Unfortunately, the government's aim in establishing the Zona Lacandona and the biosphere reserve—slowing the rate of deforestation—was not realized in the years after it was established. The roads bulldozed by the lumber companies to facilitate the extraction of timber simply opened up the forest to more rapid colonization. Because most migrants into the forest burned tracts of land to clear for farmland the rate of deforestation accelerated. Between 1976 and 1992, forest loss statewide was estimated at 50,000 to 99,000 hectares a year (O'Brien 1998:78).

In 1978, in a final attempt to protect the Lacandon forest, the government set aside 331,200 hectares of land and designated it the Montes Azules Biosphere Reserve (De Vos 1992:282). A less popular part of the government's biosphere reserve plan was the relocation of about 6,000 Tzeltal and Chol Maya living in twenty-three settlements within the new reserve's boundaries. The settlers in these non-Lacandon communities were forcibly resettled to the communities of Palestina and the newly established town of Frontera Corozal. Meanwhile, many Lacandon families who did not live within the park's boundaries were convinced to resettle in the existing communities of Lacanha, Mensäbäk, and Nahá.

The economic situation in Chiapas changed dramatically in the 1980s. In 1981, oil comprised 68.7 percent of Mexico's total exports (Cancian 1992:32). As a result, the Mexican economy was particularly vulnerable when, in 1981, the price of oil collapsed. By August 1982, the country was in an economic crisis. Mexico declared it could no longer meet its foreign debt obligations. One immediate result of this crisis was that the programs that had fueled prosperity in Chiapas for the previous decade were scaled back or canceled. As the economy collapsed and people lost their jobs, men from the highlands of Chiapas returned to farming in their home communities.

Events took a different path in the Lacandon Jungle. Because Lacandon families relied little on government-funded programs and had continued to support themselves through subsistence farming rather than wage work, the cancellation of government-sponsored programs and the loss of jobs that occurred when the economy contracted had little effect on the Lacandon. Further, Mexico's misfortune was a boon to the international tourist industry as the declining value of the peso made Mexico an even more attractive destination for tourists from Europe and the United States. As the number of visitors to Chiapas started to climb, Lacandon men spent increasing amounts of their free time at home making arts and crafts, and longer periods of time in Palenque selling these goods. Thus the decline of the oil industry, the corresponding devaluation of the peso, and inexpensive airfares for tourists all combined to help create a market for tourist goods that the Lacandon, by an accident of geography and history, found themselves in a position to fill. The Lacandon's turn to tourism was encouraged largely by factors completely beyond their understanding or control, but they were positioned to take advantage of the opportunities that expanding tourism provided.

## Family Relations and Traditional Agriculture

The Lacandon have lived and farmed in the Lacandon Jungle for at least three hundred years. In that time, their social structure and subsistence patterns became closely attuned to farming in the forest. Today, as some Lacandon become successful merchants and hire Tzeltal Maya as wage laborers to farm their *milpas*, the complex interaction between Lacandon society and agriculture is changing. To understand the transition, it is first necessary to discuss the traditional work relationships and farming practices among Lacandon families. By *traditional,* I am referring to behavior that is similar to that one would have witnessed in the late nineteenth and early twentieth centuries.

In the past, farm and household labor was typically family labor in Lacandon society, and access to a man or woman's labor was determined through kin ties and marriage. With the exception of elderly widows or those who are physically deformed, marriage is universal in Lacandon society, and a person is not considered an adult until he or she has married and started a family. Indeed, in the traditional Lacandon view people could not have a functioning household unless they were married. A man needed a wife to cook, weave, and care for children. A woman needed a man to make *milpa,* and both needed children to help care for them in their old age. The Lacandon customs that helped assign the rights to a person's labor all centered around marriage. These were the practice of polygyny, the *hetzmek* ceremony, and bride service obligations incurred by young men when they married.

As observed previously, polygyny was common in Lacandon settlements (there are only a couple remaining polygynous households today). Although Soustelle and Blom encountered few polygynous households in the camps they visited (Soustelle 1933; Blom 1944), Lacandon polygyny has been noted by visitors to their settlements for centuries. This pattern of marriage and family is well suited to subsistence farming societies where children are a valuable source of help in the *milpa* and work alongside their parents by the time they are seven or eight years old. The more children in a family, the more hands are available to work in the gardens and help with household tasks. The practice of polygyny, and the taking of child brides, meant that a man could continue fathering children into old age.

Elderly men in particular were especially dependent on their sons or sons-in-law to help with the heavy labor in a *milpa*. And when older men took young women as second and third wives and had children with these women, they could ensure a continuous supply of household help as they aged. Chan K'in Viejo, for example, fathered at least twenty-four children by three wives and had sons and sons-in-law working at his side in the *milpa* until the day he died at about the age of one hundred.

By the time they entered their teens, Lacandon adolescents had a full command of adult subsistence activities and were ready to marry. However, a young man could not marry until he had undergone his *hetzmek* or rite of passage ceremony. In this rite, the boy received ritualized instruction in adult roles and tools used in adult tasks. Young women also participated in the *hetzmek* but their marriages were not dependent on it. Some families arranged the marriage of their daughters when the girls were still small children. Chan K'in Viejo, for example, took his youngest wife into his household when she was just five or six years old. She was raised by his middle wife until she was old enough to assume the roles of an adult woman.

In other Maya groups, the *hetzmek* is performed when a child is an infant, but Lacandon fathers often delayed a son's departure (and the loss of the son's labor) by postponing the *hetzmek* until a young man's mid-teens. So while a man's strategy for maximizing the labor he received from his sons was to delay their departure from a household, daughters were married young, often in their early teens, to bring new men to work in the household.

When a young man married, the right to his labor was transferred to his father-in-law through the practice of bride service. Men traditionally began their married lives living in their father-in-law's household, and performed periods of bride service that lasted up to three years. A young man typically lived with his wife's family until the young couple had their own children. Then they would move to start their own household. In conclusion, one can see how polygyny, *hetzmek,* and bride service customs were essential social elements that helped maintain the subsistence and independent status of older men and women.

I have been discussing labor in Lacandon households. This labor was primarily organized to make *milpa,* or process the products of those *milpas.* Lacandon farmers who cultivated a traditional *milpa* planted a wide variety of root and vegetable crops. The Lacandon keep no calendar that might govern planting times. Instead, the change of seasons is marked, and planting times determined, by the flowering of specific species of forest plants which the Lacandon call the "foot" of the crop. The foot of the corn crop, as illustrated in Table 4.1, is the flowering of mahogany trees in the season *nah ya'ax k'in.*

Although a viewer's dominant impression of a *milpa* will be of corn, in the 1970s Nations and Nigh (1980) documented Lacandon farmers cultivating over seventy different plant species. Distributing a variety of plants over a *milpa,* without clustering bunches of plants together, has the practical effect of imitating the diversity and dispersal of plant life found in an undisturbed primary forest. A traditional Lacandon *milpa* thus replicates the diversity of the tropical rain forest ecosystem. The *milpa* is, in effect, a portion of jungle where Lacandon farmers concentrate a greater than normal population of food-producing crops. This concentration of food is aided by the fact that Lacandon farmers plant their *milpas* with crops that take advantage of different environmental niches within the same cleared area. For example, subsurface root crops like manioc and potatoes are cultivated below the ground's surface. At ground level, hills of corn, squash, onions, and tomatoes are sown, with bean vines climb-

TABLE 4.1    The Lacandon Seasons

| Seasonal Name | Seasonal Indicator | Months |
|---|---|---|
| *Äxpäli* "Time of the winter solstice" | Winter Solstice | December |
| *Ka-sut k'in* "Return of the sun" | Blooming of cork trees | January–February |
| *U yok'ol ya'ax k'in* "Emerging of the spring" | Mahogany trees put out leaves | March |
| *Nah ya'ax k'in* "Mother of the spring" | Mahogany trees bloom | April–May |
| *Mani ya'ax k'in* "Passing of the spring" | Mahogany trees finish blooming | June–August |
| *Bulha' k-il u tal k'in* "Flood waters from the east" | Time of the rainy season | September–October |
| *U sut äxpäli* "Return of the winter solstice time" | | November |

ing the corn stalks. Finally, a few meters above the surface, are tree crops such as bananas and oranges. Thus, a traditional Lacandon farmer achieved three levels of production from the same piece of land.

Turn of the century observers described Lacandon *milpas* as "luxuriant" (Maler 1903) and these remain so today. In 1995, 1997, and 1999, I conducted a series of *milpa* surveys in the community of Nahá and found that some farmers still cultivated a wide variety of crops. Crops I could identify are listed in Table 4.2.

**TABLE 4.2    Crops and Fruit Trees in Lacandon *Milpas* or Household Gardens, 1995**

| Lacandon Name | Translation | Use |
| --- | --- | --- |
| *Äh xux* | Garlic | Condiment |
| *Ak te?* | Lemon grass | Beverage |
| *Akum te?* | ? | Fruit |
| *Balché* | *Balché* | Ritual beverage |
| *Balum te?* | Cacao | Condiment |
| *Bambu* | Bamboo | Construction |
| *Bokempach* | Onions | Food |
| *Box* | Banana | Fruit |
| *Buul* | Beans | Food |
| *Chäk chiina* | Tangerine | Fruit |
| *Chäk chop* | Lantana | Seeds |
| *Äh chayok* | *Mal mujer* | Food |
| *Che luuch* | Gourd tree | Containers |
| *Chi* | *Nasa* | Fruit |
| *Chiina* | Orange | Fruit |
| *Chikam* | Jicama | Food |
| *Chun ak* | Passion fruit | Fruit |
| *Curanto/hon kix* | Cilantro | Condiment |
| *Hach käko* | Cacao | Condiment |
| *Ha?as* | Mamey | Fruit |
| *Ik* | Chili | Food |
| *Is* | Sweet potato | Food |
| *Isum te?* | ? | Food wrapper |
| *Käx ex* | Goose foot | Condiment |
| *K?um* | Squash | Food |

Items marked with question marks are those that I am not conclusively able to identify.

Although I no longer find the seventy-nine crops that Nations and Nigh (1980) found in the 1970s, traditional-style Lacandon *milpas* are far more productive than the fields of Indians from surrounding communities. Yield estimates compiled by Nations and Komer (1982:10) for the Lacandon demonstrate the effective-

| Lacandon Name | Translation | Use |
|---|---|---|
| K'uxu | Achiote | Condiment, dye |
| Lek | Squash gourd | Container |
| Luch | Squash gourd | Container |
| Mäkäl | Malanga | Food |
| Melon | Canteloupe | Fruit |
| Mulix | Lime | Fruit |
| Näl | Maize | Food |
| On | Avocado | Food |
| Op | Annona | Fruit |
| Pach | Pineapple | Fruit |
| P'ak | Cherry tomato | Food |
| Pap u wi | Ginger | Condiment |
| Päpox | Custard apple | Fruit |
| Paytam | Plantain | Fruit |
| P'iix | Chayote | Food |
| Pichik, p'ul | Guava | Fruit |
| Popox | Guayabana | Fruit |
| Puham | Chokecherry | Fruit |
| P'uut | Papaya | Fruit |
| Säk wool | Canna lily | Food wrapper |
| Sandia | Watermelon | Fruit |
| Sikil | Squash | Food |
| Sulí | Yam | Food |
| Tsakax | Mint | Condiment |
| Tsin | Manioc | Food |

ness of traditional Lacandon cultivation techniques. *Milpas* of traditional Lacandon farmers produced about 6.5 tons of shelled corn per hectare per year and an equal amount of root and vegetable crops. In comparison, the Tzotzil Maya community of Nuevo San Juan Chamula, composed of immigrants from the highlands, produced 1.4 metric tons of shelled corn per hectare, far less than the Lacandon yield (Preciado 1976, quoted in Nations and Nigh 1980:13). Although some of this difference can be explained by soil quality and other environmental factors, the newcomers' lack of experience in rain forest farming, and some communities' focus on cattle and cash cropping is also a factor. Additionally, the immigrant Maya farmers in the area typically cultivate a *milpa* for only two years. In contrast, traditional crop rotation and soil management techniques allow Lacandon farmers to use the same field for up to eight years.

A fallowed *milpa,* or *pak che kol* (literally "planted tree *milpa*"), is also an important resource for Lacandon farmers. While *pak che kol* are not actively cultivated, Lacandon farmers do not abandon them. Fruit trees are maintained in deserted *milpas* and farmers continue to harvest leftover crops and species of wild plants from them. Furthermore, there is preliminary evidence that traditional Lacandon farmers manage their *pak che kol* by encouraging the growth of certain wild plants, and that regeneration of the soil occurs more quickly than in the *milpas* of other Maya groups (Ron Nigh 1996: personal communication).

A fallowed *milpa* also attracts game animals because there is a greater concentration of food sources than in the surrounding jungle. Although the number of game animals such as deer, javelina, and peccary have declined in the last few decades, the abandoned *milpa* attracts them and makes it easier for Lacandon hunters to supplement their diets with animal protein.

Having lovingly described traditional *milpa* agriculture, I must acknowledge that this type of production is in decline. Traditional farming practices are not compatible with full-time production of arts and crafts, and crop variety is declining in even the best *milpas*. Many families today ignore *milpa* farming and concentrate on producing and selling arts and crafts. Families in Nahá who have made an investment in the tourist industry have had to adapt their agricultural practices to the demands of craft production. To a large degree this means they do not make *milpa*. For the most part, these families have accommodated their desire to earn cash though the sale of arts and crafts by hiring Tzeltal Maya from nearby communities to clear fields and plant corn and beans for them.

# Roads, Bows and Arrows, and Tourism

In the summer of 1980, a road connecting Nahá with Palenque, and ultimately ending in Ocosingo, was bulldozed through the jungle. I watched the construction of this road, and at the time, had no way of knowing that it would establish a dividing line between traditional subsistence-oriented living and today's commercial enterprises. It was a turning point in Lacandon history.

In their forest home, the Lacandon were never completely isolated from the outside world. For several centuries, the Lacandon have conducted business with the people of Palenque, trading corn, tobacco, cotton, and cacao for axes, knives, and machetes. In the early part of the twentieth century, trading of bows and arrows, tobacco, and honey was common. These were bartered for other subsistence items, in particular, salt, cloth, and metal tools. I have already described, for example, how Maler was accompanied back to the *montería* of Tinieblas by Lacandon men intent on trade. However, before the road, Lacandon commercial transactions were limited by geography and lack of transportation. If a man wanted to sell bows and arrows, he packed as many as he could carry on his back and walked to the towns of Ocosingo, Tenosique, or Palenque. Chan K'in Viejo, for instance, reminisced about how, as a young man, he would pack as much tobacco and bow and arrows as he could carry and hike for three days to Tenosique. Once there he would sell his goods and buy salt and machetes to take back home. Because these trips required days of hard hiking through mountainous terrain and camping in the forest, contact with the outside world was intermittent and trade was limited by the volume of material a man could carry.

The construction of the road into the forest changed the fundamental relationship between the elements that had limited Lacandon trade since the eighteenth century. With the opening of the road and the beginning of regular vehicular transportation through the Lacandon Jungle, a man from Nahá could move large quantities of crafts directly to cities where there were large numbers of tourists. A Lacandon man interested in earning cash for household goods no longer had to walk for days to reach his market. Additionally, the volume of material a man could carry was no longer a limiting factor. Men literally began constructing tourist goods by the truckload.

While the Lacandon also sell clay figures, necklaces made from seeds, and other crafts, the majority of their income comes from the sale of bows and arrows. The Lacandon hunted with these weapons as recently as the 1940s when the archeologist Franz Blom and his wife collected several sets. However, the sets the Lacandon make and sell today are really toys, made from different materials than the traditional hunting bows.

Lacandon men and women make bow and arrow sets in a variety of sizes, from a full-sized hunting set to a child-size toy. Prices of these sets are based on their size and the number of arrows they contain. In the summer of 1997, the smallest sets were 40 pesos ($5.15 U.S.); medium sets, 50 pesos ($6.40 U.S.); and large sets, 60 pesos ($7.70 U.S.).

Bows are usually made from the wood of the chicle tree and shaped with a machete. The bowstrings are typically cord made from the braided fibers of the agave plant. The arrows are composed of cane shafts called *oh*, or *carrizo* in Spanish, a bamboo-like domesticated grass. Arrow foreshafts are typically whittled from tropical cedar or sapodilla wood. They are sharpened to a point on one end and that end is inserted into the hollow cane shaft. The other end is notched to fit the arrow point. Projectile points are usually made from locally available chert that is knapped using indirect percussion and then pressure flaked into a point with a piece of broken machete blade. Fletching for the arrows is typically dove or chicken feathers that are painted bright colors to resemble the plumage of tropical birds. The fletching and arrow points are attached to the arrow shaft with cotton string that has been rubbed with a mix of wax and black soot from the resin of pitch pine. The black twine provides a strong binding that is also used as a decorative wrap on the arrow shafts (for more on Lacandon arrows, see Nations and Clark 1983). One recent change in arrow production is that instead of acquiring materials from the forest and making the arrows themselves, some men buy all the materials for their bows and arrows and concentrate only on assembling the pieces.

Bow and arrow sets are sold directly to tourists visiting the ancient Maya ruins at Palenque, or at a discounted price to shop owners in the city of San Cristobal who resell them. The profits in bow and arrow sales can be quite high and young Lacandon men, in particular, produce them in large numbers. For instance, in October 1981, Koh III's son K'in (#18) had accumulated three hundred arrows and was making bows to go with them. At the same time, one of K'in's closet friends, a son of Matejo Viejo, had completed fifty bow and arrow sets and was planning to sell them for up to 300 pesos a set. Two months later, I encountered several young Lacandon men in Palenque who were selling bows and arrows at the ruins. K'in (#9) was there with one hundred bow and arrow sets to sell; his younger brother Kayum (#14) had fifty sets. By August the following year, K'in (#9) was back in Palenque with two hundred more sets to sell. This pattern has continued up to the present. In June 1997, Chan K'in Viejo's son Kayum (#23) was working full-time to stockpile bows and arrows for sale in August. That summer, Kayum had bought one hundred pieces of wood to make bows for 50 pesos. He had also purchased materials to make arrows (a bag of projectile points, a roll of string for fastening the arrows, and a box of paints for decorating feathers) for about 150 pesos. He hoped to sell the finished bow and arrow sets for about 2,400 pesos (about $300 U.S.). Thus for an initial expenditure of about $25 U.S. in materials, Kayum would make $300 U.S. in sales.

Over the course of the twenty years I have worked with the Lacandon, I have observed men selling bows and arrows outside the ruins of Palenque many times (see Figure 4.1). In June of 1997, for instance, tourism was slow. Lingering fears about the Zapatista uprising kept visitors to a minimum and many men were stockpiling stores of goods in Nahá in anticipation of the August vacation rush. Nonetheless, sales at the ruins were profitable. On one occasion a single group of tourists bought over 1,000 pesos ($128 U.S.) worth of Lacandon crafts in less than ten minutes. On busy days, I have seen Lacandon vendors earn up to 1,300 pesos ($160–$170 U.S.) a day. Sales of 300 to 400 pesos ($40–$50 U.S.) constituted a slow day. Although some of their profit is spent to support themselves in Palenque, industrious people earn surprisingly large sums of money. K'in, for example, is one of the few Lacandon who has given up the forest and lives full-time in Palenque with his family selling crafts to tourists. He rents an

FIGURE 4.1    Selling bows and arrows at Palenque.

apartment for 400 pesos a month (about $51 U.S. in 1997) and pays about another 100 pesos (roughly $13 U.S.) for electricity and water. Thus in an average day of sales during the peak tourist season K²in can pay for his rent and utilities. A couple good days more would take care of his family's food expenses for the month.

K²in's case is not typical because he lives in Palenque permanently and supports his family with his sales. Most Lacandon families prefer to stay in their home communities. The income they generate selling tourist goods is typically used for entertainment systems, household utensils, prepackaged or processed foods, and cookies and soft drinks. Even in 1980, all families owned items such as *molinos* (metal corn grinders), portable radios, pots and pans, and plastic dishes. Today, virtually all the householders in Nahá earn enough money to equip their homes with color televisions, videocassette recorders, and stereos. Four families possess satellite dishes.

The downside to the trade in tourist goods, of course, is that an income generated by tourism is dependent on tourists. When tourism is slow, there is no market for bows and arrows and no profits for those families trying to sell them. For example, between 1996 and 1999 I visited with several families who concentrated on tourism and invested little time in their *milpas*. By May and June, they had run out of corn, a couple months before the next crop was ready for harvest. These families were thus forced to spend the bulk of their tourist income on corn or *Maseca*, an instant tortilla mix, because they had run out of food. Similarly, K?in (#9), a successful vendor in 1997, sought me out in Palenque to borrow money to pay for a family member's medical care in May 2001. In a slow tourist season he was barely able to make ends meet.

In the early 1980s, I considered the Lacandon's ability to generate incomes a positive response to the uncertainties of an agricultural lifestyle (McGee 1990). For instance, because he had a cash income Chan K?in Viejo was able to purchase the maize harvest of a man in Mensäbäk when his own crop failed in a drought. In June of 1997, however, the most dramatic consequence of some Lacandon families' full-time investment in tourism was that they had run out of corn several months before the new corn would be ready for harvest. Literally, all the households in Nahá whose members hired Tzeltal laborers to work their fields so that they could concentrate on the full-time manufacture and sale of tourists goods had run out of corn. They were either buying corn from stores in neighboring communities or living on store-bought tortilla mix. As the pattern became clear, I remember thinking how ironic it was that in the land where corn was first domesticated, the farmers who could produce 13,000 pounds of shelled corn per hectare using only axes and machetes had abandoned those techniques and were subsisting on powdered tortilla mixes. On one hand, the conclusion I reached in 1982 and 1983 is true. The income families earn gives them the flexibility to buy food when crops are bad. However, when one's primary subsistence investment is in tourist goods, what do you do when tourism is down? If a family has not planted a *milpa* and cannot make money in the tourist trade they can end up with no way to feed themselves. If they plant a *milpa*, even in a bad year they will have food on the table even if they do not have the extra cash to buy a television.

# Adapting Agriculture to Tourism: Comparing Two Communities

Only a few Lacandon families sell their arts and crafts on a year-round, full-time basis. Most spend only a few weeks at a time in Palenque or San Cristobal, earning enough money to last a few months, before returning home. This form of part-time vending of tourist goods does not necessarily compete with traditional-style agriculture. Peak tourist season in Palenque is August and December–January. Because corn planting typically occurs in April–May, the man who goes to Palenque to sell crafts in August misses only a few weeks of weeding. January is the time of year when men start clearing land for *milpas*. Because most men now hire Tzeltal workers to do this arduous work, a Lacandon man can spend the December holiday season in Palenque and still continue to work his *milpa*.

The cost of a day's labor in the Lacandon Jungle in 1999 was about 50 pesos per day (between $5 and $6 U.S.). Consequently, if a Lacandon vendor can earn $160 U.S. in a good day of arrow sales, he can purchase almost a month's worth of full-time labor. As a result, even the eldest and most traditional of households, men such as Chan K'in Viejo and Matejo Viejo, were seasonally engaged in the bow and arrow trade. However, it is clear that in Nahá these profits come at a price. There is a direct relationship between the size and variety of a family's *milpa* and the degree of their involvement in the tourist trade.

## Agriculture and Tourism in Nahá

There are about two hundred people in Nahá today, with an almost even number of men and women. Of the ninety males in the community, forty-one were the adult heads of households. Of these, only five were farming in the traditional style in 1997. Of the five traditional farming households, all were headed by men over forty, and in two cases the heads of the household were over sixty. Three households were run by older widowed women. These three households also continued to farm in the traditional manner. Thus in 1997, only eight out of forty-four households in

Nahá were growing the customary variety of crops in a traditional-style *milpa*.

At the time, I was struck by the generational division between those who farmed in the traditional manner and those who did not. As I looked at my charts it seemed clear that young men in Nahá had abandoned traditional *milpa* farming in order to work full-time selling arts and crafts to tourists. Surveys of twenty five *milpas* in Nahá in the summer of 1997 clearly demonstrated this generational change. Table 4.3 shows a sample of these surveys comparing the crops grown by men and women of different age groups. The table shows clearly that the youngest generation of adult men seemed to have abandoned any pretense of traditional farming and hired Tzeltal Maya day laborers to grow only corn and beans.

By the time I started surveying *milpas* in 1995, crop variety had declined in even the best of them. Compared to the Lacandon fields surveyed in the 1970s, when farmers raised as many as seventy-nine different crops (Nigh and Nations 1980), the variety of food crops planted by traditional farmers has declined as much as 50 percent. Although most of the items found in Nations and Nigh's *milpa* inventory can still be found they are no longer universally planted. Table 4.3 lists the total number of plants that I found in my survey of twenty-five *milpas*. Out of a total of sixty-five different plants identified in all Lacandon *milpas* in the summer of 1997, no one *milpa* contained more than thirty. However, this drop looks insignificant when compared to the decline in plant diversity in the fields owned by young men who hired neighboring Tzeltal Maya to clear and plant their *milpas*. The fields of these young men contain at most only two crops, typically corn and beans or corn and squash.

Further, unlike the random and diverse planting of the eldest farmers, in 1997 many young men's *milpas* were planted in rows to facilitate the spraying of herbicides. This makes economic sense in that agrochemicals reduce the number of days required for *milpa* work, in particular weeding, thus minimizing the amount a household must pay to hire day labor. However, these chemicals are sprayed indiscriminately and without protective equipment opening up the possibility of contamination of other food crops and accidental poisoning.

**TABLE 4.3  Diversity in Lancandon Milpas by Generation, 1997**

| Lacandon | English | Male 60+ | Male 60+ | Female 60+ | Female 60+ | Male 40+ | Male 40+ | Male 40+ | Male 40+ | Male 40+ | Male 40+ | Male 30–40 | Male 30 | Male 30 | Male 20–30 | Male 20–30 | Male 20–30 |
|---|---|---|---|---|---|---|---|---|---|---|---|---|---|---|---|---|---|
| Ahbon | Fruit? | | | | | | | | X | | | | | | | | |
| Ak | Lemon grass | | | | | | | | | | | | | | | | |
| Akum le? | Fruit? | | | | | | | X | | | | | | | | | |
| Anise | Anise | | | | | | | | | | | | | | | | |
| Asucar | Sugarcane | X | | X | | X | X | | | | | | | | | | |
| Äh xux | Garlic | | X | | X | X | X | X | | | | | | | | | |
| Bäk nikte | Plumeria | | X | X | X | | | | | | | | | | | | |
| Balché | Balche | | | | | | | | | | | | | | | | |
| Bitts | Fruit | | | X | | | | | | | | | | | | | |
| Box | Banana | X | X | X | | X | | X | | | | | | | | | |
| Box buul | Banana beans? | | | X | X | | | | | | | | | | | | |
| Buul (chäk) | Red beans | | | X | X | | | | | | | | | | | | |
| Buul (ek) | Black beans | X | | X | X | X | X | X | | | | | | X | | | |
| Cafe | Coffee | | X | | | | | | | | | | | | | | |
| Cahcuate | Peanuts | | | X | | | | | | | | | | | | | |
| Chäk chiina | Tangerine | | | X | X | | | | | | | | | | | | |
| Chäk chob | Lantana | X | X | X | X | | X | X | | | | | | | | | |
| Chayok | Mal mujer | | X | X | | X | X | | | | | | | | | | |
| Cebolla | Onions | | X | X | | X | X | X | | | | | | | | | |
| Chiina | Orange | | X | | X | X | X | X | | | | | | | | | |
| Chikäm | Jicama | | | | | | | | | | | | | | | | |
| Chun aaki | Passion fruit | | | | | | | | | | | | | | | | |
| Chankalah | For necklaces | | | X | X | X | | X | | | | | | | | | |
| Curanto | Cilantro/ coriander | | | X | X | X | | | | | | | | | | | |
| Ip | Lima beans? | X | X | X | X | X | | X | | | | | | | | | |
| Ik | Chili peppers | | X | X | X | X | X | X | | | | | | | | | |
| Is | Yam | X | X | X | X | | X | X | | | | | | | | | |
| K'ik' | Rubber | | X | | | | | | | | | | | | | | |
| Kulix | Repollo (large onion) | | X | | | | | | | | | | | | | | |
| K?um | Squash | X | X | X | X | X | | X | | | | | | | X | | |
| Kun | Spined salt palm | | X | | | X | X | | | | | | | | | | |
| Ah ku'ut? | ? | | | X | | | | | | | | | | | | | |
| K'uuts | Tobacco | X | X | | X | | X | | | | | | | | | | |
| K'ixu | Achiote | | | X | | X | | X | | | | | | | | | |

*(continued)*

**TABLE 4.3**  *(continued)*

| Lacandon | English | Male 60+ | Male 60+ | Female 60+ | Female 60+ | Male 40+ | Male 40+ | Male 40+ | Male 40+ | Male 40+ | Male 40+ | Male 30–40 | Male 30 | Male 30 | Male 20–30 | Male 20–30 | Male 20–30 |
|---|---|---|---|---|---|---|---|---|---|---|---|---|---|---|---|---|---|
| *Lechuga* | Greens ? | X | | | | | | | | | | | | | | | |
| *Lek* | Squash gourd | | | | X | | | | | X | | | | | | | |
| *Luch* | Squash gourd | | | | X | | | | | | | | | | | | |
| *Mäkäl* | Malanga | | | | X | | X | X | X | X | | | | | | | |
| *Mulix* | Lime | | | | | | X | X | | X | | | | | | | |
| *Näl (säk)* | White maize | X | | X | X | X | X | X | X | X | X | X | X | X | X | X | X |
| *Näl (kän)* | Yellow maize | | | X | X | | | | X | | | | | | | X | |
| *Oh* | Reeds for arrows | | X | X | X | | | | | X | X | X | | | X | | |
| *On* | Avocado | | | X | X | | X | X | | X | | | | | | | |
| *Op* | Annona | | | | | | | X | | | | | | | | | |
| *Pach* | Pineapple | | | X | | | | X | X | | | | | X | | | |
| *P'ak* | Cherry tomato | | X | X | | | | X | X | X | | | | X | | | |
| *Pak yom* | "Homa"-like chiib | | X | | | | | | | | | | | | | | |
| *Popox* | Guayabana | | | X | X | | | X | X | X | | | | | | | |
| *Paytam* | Plantain | | X | X | | | | X | X | X | | | | X | | | |
| *Pedejil* | Parsley | | | | X | | | | | | | | | | | | |
| *P'iix* | Chayote | X | | | X | | | | X | | | | | | | | |
| *Puham* | Chokecherry | | | | | | | | X | | | | | | | | |
| *P'uut* | Papaya | | X | | | | | | | | | | | | | | |
| *Sak uh* | Seeds for necklace | | | X | X | | | | | X | | | | | | | |
| *Säk wohel* | Canna lily | X | | X | | | | X | | X | | | | X | | | |
| *Sandia* | Watermelon | | X | X | | | | | | | | | | | | | |
| *Siki te che'* | Physic nut | | | X | | | | | | | | | | | | | |
| *Siki te lu'um* | ? | | | X | | | | | | | | | | | | | |
| *Tämän* | Cotton | | X | X | X | | | | | X | X | | | X | | | |
| *Tsin (hach)* | Manioc | | | X | X | | | | | X | | | | X | | | |
| *Tsin (ya'ax)* | Green manioc | | | X | | | | | X | | | | | X | | | |
| *Tsin (chäk)* | Red manioc | | | | | | | | X | | | | | | | | |
| *Tsuli* | Jicama | | | X | | | | | | | | | | | | | |
| *Tuch* | Tree fruit | | X | | X | | | | | X | | | | | | | |

Items marked with question marks are those that I am not conclusively able to identify.

Young men I interviewed were not bothered by the differences between their *milpas* and those of their fathers. Not only were they spared the hard manual labor required in making *milpa*, but they were also paid to grow corn through a government subsidy program called the Programa Nacional de Apoyos Directos al Campo (PROCAMPO). In 1997, PROCAMPO paid farmers in the Lacandon Jungle 2,000 pesos per hectare of corn under cultivation (about $256 U.S.). That summer, 2,000 pesos was enough money to hire a Tzeltal Maya laborer for 40 to 50 days of field work per hectare (see Figure 4.2). Thus the PROCAMPO program actually encouraged young men to invest their time in the tourist industry. The PROCAMPO money allowed Lacandon men to have their corn grown for them virtually free while they concentrated on craft production.

In 1997, I feared that one result of the commercial success of young Lacandon men was that in hiring Tzeltal and Tzotzil Maya to work their *milpas* they were perpetuating the agricultural practices that promoted soil erosion, nutrient depletion, and the spread of pesticides and herbicides in areas surrounding the Lacandon forest. I thought I had found a relationship between the Lacandon's success in the marketplace, newfound ability to hire labor,

**FIGURE 4.2**    Tzeltal Maya planting a Lacandon *milpa*, 1995.

and the degradation of the subsistence practices and environment that had sustained them for centuries. I was convinced that tourism was leading to the demise of traditional Lacandon agriculture. However, when I returned to Nahá in 1999 I was astonished to find that several of the young men I had watched making bows and arrows in 1997 were cultivating beautiful *milpas*. The generational differences in *milpa* farming had been so clear and dramatic in 1997 that I was surprised to find young men farming. I realized that the Lacandon were much more sophisticated in their manipulation of subsistence strategies than I had previously imagined. I discovered that local conditions had conspired to create income-producing opportunities in Nahá itself, so that young men could earn money without leaving the community. Staying in Nahá gave these men the time and opportunity to produce their own *milpas*.

Until 1999, I had expected Lacandon men to either make *milpa* or sell bows and arrows. My experience in 1999 led me to realize that all but the oldest Lacandon men and women change subsistence strategies according to local conditions and decide what activities will have the best payoff for them in the upcoming year. In 1997, PROCAMPO payments paid for the Tzeltal labor needed to grow corn, so many young Lacandon men felt that they had an opportunity to earn substantial profits selling arts and crafts in Palenque without sacrificing their corn crop. In 1999, forest fires in Chiapas slowed tourism but created an opportunity for earning money locally that also allowed several men to stay home and make *milpa*.

The fires that swept through the area in April and May of 1999 did a lot of damage. Instead of the green on green on green that I was used to seeing when I walked out the door of my house, I saw brown, charred, hillsides. However, even in disaster there is opportunity. I discovered that many young men in the community were self-employed collecting seeds and selling them to the state forestry personnel in charge of reseeding areas of burned forest. Kayum (#23), Chan K'in (#24), and K'in (#25), for example, were all collecting seeds and selling them for 200 pesos a kilo. Additionally, Kayum and a friend were selling a fruit they collected called *wäch*, or wild tamarind, that grew near their *milpas*. They sold this fruit in neighboring villages for 300 pesos per kilo. At the same time, their mothers had grown large quantities of tobacco that they were selling for 100 pesos a kilo. Thus there was ample opportunity in the spring and summer of 1999 to earn money without going to Palenque to sell arts and crafts.

Given an opportunity to make money at home in Nahá rather than Palenque, I found that many young men chose to spend their time making *milpa* rather than bows and arrows. Three of the young men listed in Table 4.3 who I found planting only corn in 1997 had thriving *milpas* in 1999. Although they still had not planted the variety of crops found in the *milpas* of sixty- and seventy-year-old Lacandon farmers, what I found was a far cry from the single-crop *milpas* of 1997. In 1999, I found the crops shown in Table 4.4 under cultivation in the *milpas* of the same twenty- to thirty-year-old men I surveyed in 1997.

In addition to the economic situation, political factors also encouraged young men to stay home and make *milpa* in the spring of 1999. Since the Zapatista uprising in 1994, settlements of indigenous Zapatista supporters have sprung up on privately owned land in the Ocosingo Valley and in the forest surrounding the land deeded to the Lacandon by the Mexican government. The Lacandon I know are neutral in this conflict. Although Maya in the highlands of Chiapas have suffered discrimination and exploitation for centuries, the Lacandon have received benign treatment from the state and national governments in recent years and do not support the Zapatista cause. Unlike Zapatista supporters in the highlands of Chiapas, the Lacandon have title to large areas of forest. Because they are few in number, the Lacandon have access to plenty of farmland. However, as Zapatista communities have sprung up in the forest there have been numerous cases of Lacandon land and crops being appropriated by force or other forms of harassment, such as men riding their horses through Lacandon *milpas* and trampling the crops. In 1997, for example,

**TABLE 4.4    Young Men's Crops in 1999**

| | | | |
|---|---|---|---|
| *Box* | Bananas | *P'iix* | Chayote |
| *Näl* | Corn | *Mäkäl* | *Malanga* |
| *Ek buul* | Black beans | *Is* | Sweet potato |
| *Cebolla* | Onions | *P'ak* | Cherry tomato |
| *Kum* | Squash | *Suli* | Yams |
| *Paytam* | Plantain | | |

K?in (#18) was ordered off one of his *milpas* at gunpoint by men from the community of Jardin. At a meeting between men from Nahá and Jardin that spring, one member of the Jardinero group stated that because they were armed and more numerous they could kill anyone who resisted them.

In addition to requests for aid from the governor's office in Tuxtla, the local response of young Lacandon men was to make new *milpas* on the eastern border of the land between Nahá and Jardin. This served to mark the people of Nahá's ownership of the land and negate anyone else's claim that the land was abandoned and unused. Many of the young men who made *milpa* in the spring of 1999, rather than sell bows and arrows, were helping defend their community's claim to Lacandon land. In the spring of 2001, men from the community of Jardin once again invaded and began clearing land belonging to the people of Nahá. It took the direct intervention of the governor of Chiapas, and a promise of aid from the state, to convince the Jardineros to leave Lacandon land.

In sum, what I have learned in three years of surveying *milpas* and counting bow and arrow sales is that the Lacandon have a practical, multiuse, multigeneration subsistence strategy to support their households. Virtually all households, young or old, sell some arts and crafts. Older men and women concentrate on making *milpa*, but manufacture or help make tourist crafts in their spare time. The young men of the family then sell these crafts. Middle-aged and young married couples tend to focus less on traditional-style agriculture and work together to make bows and arrows and clay figures. If a couple does not want to leave Nahá, they sell their crafts to other Lacandon who are willing to spend time in Palenque. However, if local conditions provide the opportunity to make an income in or around Nahá, most families are happy to stay in Nahá, concentrate on farming, and earn cash in their spare time by selling tobacco, eggs, materials for making bows and arrows, or forest products, such as seeds and fruits.

In conclusion, when it is profitable to stay in Nahá, people stay in Nahá and farm in a more traditional style. When the tourist market is strong younger families are more likely to invest greater amounts of time and energy making arts and crafts to sell in Palenque and hire Tzeltal Maya day laborers to grow corn for them. In general, the tourist business is a young person's game;

as they age, Lacandon men are less interested in Palenque's glamour and are more likely to stay home, tend their *milpas*, and help their sons make crafts to sell.

## Agriculture and Tourism in Lacanha

The idea that agricultural diversity is inversely related to investment in the tourist industry is supported by the relationship between agriculture and commerce that I observed among Northern Lacandon in the predominantly Southern Lacandon community of Lacanha. In the summer of 1999, I took a group of students to Lacanha. We stayed in a small enclave of Northern Lacandon who had relatives in Nahá and had the opportunity to survey their *milpas* and assess the volume of goods they produced for tourists. In terms of commerce with tourists, the position of people in Lacanha is much stronger than that of the people of Nahá. If you live in Nahá and want to sell crafts to tourists you have to arrange transport to Palenque over a one-lane dirt road, rent lodging, and buy food during your stay there. It is difficult to make a decent *milpa* if you plan to spend a long time in Palenque.

Lacanha, on the other hand, is a popular tourist destination reached by paved highway. The community is advantageously located near the ancient Maya site of Bonampak, which is famous for the murals preserved in one of the structures. Additionally, Lacanha is only a few minutes' detour for those more intrepid tourists who plan to boat up the Usumacinta River to visit the Classic Period Maya city of Yaxchilan. In other words, the people of Lacanha do not have to travel to Palenque to find tourists. The tourists come to them by the busload. Several Lacandon families even have rudimentary facilities for people who want to camp.

Given the volume of tourists that visit Lacanha I expected to find a large variety of arts and crafts being produced there. Also, I guessed that since the Lacandon in Lacanha do not have to stay in Palenque to sell arts and crafts to tourists they would have more time to invest in their *milpas* and would produce a greater variety of crops. This is exactly what I found. In several households I encountered whole rooms devoted to storing tourist goods. But members of these households were also cultivating bountiful *milpas*. Table 4.5 lists the *milpa* crops cultivated by the Northern Lacandon men we visited in Lacanha.

**TABLE 4.5    Crops Cultivated in Lacanha**

| Lacandon | English | Male 60+ | Male 60+ | Male 40+ | Male 40+ |
|---|---|---|---|---|---|
| *Ahbon* | Fruit (plum ?) | | | | |
| *Äh xux* | Garlic | | | | |
| *Ak* | Lemon grass | | | | |
| *Akum te* | Fruit ? | | | | X |
| *Almendra* | Almond tree | | | X | |
| *Asucar* | Sugarcane | X | | | X |
| *Bäk nikte* | Plumeria | | | | |
| *Blaché* | *Balché* | | | | |
| *Biits* | Fruit | | | | |
| *Box* | Banana | X | X | X | X |
| *Box buul* | Banana beans ? | | | | |
| *Buul (chäk)* | Red beans | | | | |
| *Buul (ek)* | Black beans | | | | |
| *Cafe* | Coffee | | | | |
| *Cachuate* | Peanuts | | | | |
| *Chäk chiina* | Tangerine | | X | | |
| *Chäk chob* | Lantana | | | | X |
| *Chaya* | Chaya | | X | | X |
| *Chayok* | *Mal mujer* | | | | |
| *Cebolla* | Onions | X | X | X | X |
| *Chiina* | Orange | X | X | | X |
| *Chikäm* | Jicama | | | X | |
| *Chun aaki* | Passion fruit | | X | | X |
| *Chankalah* | For necklaces | X | X | | X |
| *Coco* | Coconut | X | X | | X |
| *Curanto* | Cilantro/coriander | X | | | X |
| *Hon kix* | Cilantro/coriander | | | X | |
| *Ip* | Lima bean ? | | | X | |
| *Ik* | Chili peppers | X | X | X | X |
| *Is* | Yam | X | | X | X |
| *Käkäwat* | Peanuts | | | | X |
| *Ki* | Agave/hennquen | | X | | |
| *K'ik'* | Rubber | | | | |
| *Kulix* | *Repollo* (large onion) | | | | |
| *Kum* | Squash | X | X | X | X |
| *Kun* | Spined salt palm | | | | |

*(continued)*

TABLE 4.5    *(continued)*

| Lacandon | English | Male 60+ | Male 60+ | Male 40+ | Male 40+ |
|---|---|---|---|---|---|
| *Ah ku'ut* | ? | | | | |
| K'uuts | Tobacco | X | X | | X |
| K'uxu | Achiote | X | | | |
| Lechuga | Greens ? | | | | |
| Lek | Squash gourd | X | | | |
| Luch | Squash gourd | X | | | |
| Mäkäl | *Malanga* | X | X | X | X |
| Mulix | Lime | X | | | X |
| Näl (säk) | White maize | X | X | X | X |
| Näl (kän) | Yellow maize | | | | |
| Oh | Reeds for arrows | | | | |
| On | Avocado | | | | |
| Op | *Annona* | X | | | X |
| Pach | Pineapple | | | | |
| P'ak | Cherry tomato | X | X | X | X |
| Pak yom | "Homa"-like chiib | | | | |
| Papox | Guayabana | | | | |
| Paytam | Plantain | | | | X |
| Pedejii | Parsley | | | | |
| Pesa | Ginger | | X | | |
| Pichik | Guava | | | | X |
| P'iix | Chayote | | | | X |
| Puham | Chokecherry | | | X | X |
| P'uut | Papaya | X | | X | X |
| Säk uh | Seeds for necklace | | | | X |
| Säk wohel | Canna lily | | | | |
| Sandia | Watermelon | X | | | X |
| Siki te ché | Physic nut | X | X | | |
| Tämän | Cotton | | X | | |
| Tsikil | Pumpkin | | X | | |
| Tsin (hach) | Manioc | X | X | X | |
| Tsin (ya'ax) | Green manioc | X | | | X |
| Tsin (chäk) | | | | | X |
| Tsuli | Jicama | | | | X |
| Tuch | Tree fruit | | | | |
| Yali che' | Jamaica | | | | X |

Items marked with question marks are those that I am not conclusively able to identify.

TABLE 4.6    Tourists Goods Sold by a Lacandon Household
in Lacanha

| Item | Price in Pesos | U.S. Dollars |
|------|----------------|--------------|
| Bows and arrows | 100 | $11 |
| Wooden figures | 50, 70, 80 | $5.50, $7.70, $8.90 |
| Drums | 50, 70 | $5.50, $7.70 |
| Clay jaguars | 50 | $5.50 |
| Clay human figures | 50 | $5.50 |
| Clay toucans | 30 | $3.30 |
| *Chuyu²* | 40, 70 | $4.40, $7.70 |
| Wooden spoons | 30 | $3.30 |
| Gourd rattles | 20 | $2.20 |
| God pots | 30 | $3.30 |
| Necklaces | 20 | $2.20 |

Table 4.6 lists the types of tourist crafts these men were manufacturing and selling. Vicente, for example, was cultivating a
*milpa* in which I counted thirty different crops. At the same time,
he had the greatest variety of tourist goods I had ever seen in a Lacandon household. He said that when he was in the *milpa* his wife
worked on crafts for tourists.

In addition to the goods they made for tourists, the men in
this house compound were cultivating fields of chili peppers to
sell. Chilies, along with coffee and cacao, are one of the primary
cash crops cultivated in Chiapas and that summer they planned
to sell ten-kilo bags of chilies for about 100 pesos per bag. I do not
know how the crop turned out, or how much money these men
made, but it is clear they were taking advantage of a variety of
strategies to maximize their incomes.

I said earlier that for a Lacandon in Palenque, a very good
day's sales would be about 1,300 pesos. It is clear that Vicente and
his comrades could probably equal that volume without leaving
their homes or *milpas.*

As the example of Vicente makes apparent, the Lacandon of
Nahá enter the tourist industry at the expense of the quantity
and variety of crops they plant. In Nahá, one cannot invest
large amounts of time in the tourist trade and still maintain a

high-quality *milpa*. Those who spend large amounts of time in Palenque selling crafts typically hire Tzeltal to plant corn and beans for them and usually end the agricultural year buying corn or tortilla mix as their own stocks of food dwindle. Those who invest a small amount of time in the tourist trade and sell their crafts during off periods in the agricultural cycle typically farm in a more traditional style and consequently produce more food. It is only in a situation where large numbers of tourists come to a community allowing men to sell their crafts at home, as one sees in Lacanha, that you find both bountiful *milpas* and the marketing of large quantities of arts and crafts.

# Women, Tourism, and Work

## Traditional Women

The extent to which Lacandon women are involved in the new tourist-based economy is largely determined by the primary subsistence activity of the men in their households. Women who live in households with men who farm in the traditional manner generally adhere to the traditional tasks of Lacandon women. Widows who must support themselves and their dependents do so by engaging in a mixed farming–commercial economy. Young married women whose husbands are active in the trade to tourists typically help their husbands assemble bows and arrows, make their own crafts, and manage their household's finances.

The lives of young Lacandon women can be radically altered by their husband's choice of subsistence farming or commerce in tourist goods. When the work of their husbands and fathers is no longer focused on producing corn, women's lives no longer revolve around processing corn. The use of tortilla mixes such as *Maseca* eliminates the hours that women must spend daily shelling and grinding corn. By the turn of the twentieth century Lacandon families had the money to buy cloth, so that women no longer spent hours in front of their looms or spinning thread. Today, in the time freed up by not grinding corn or weaving, women help their husbands make bows and arrows. Many women also specialize in the manufacture of clay figures, net bags, necklaces, and other items their husbands sell to tourists (for more about Lacandon women's roles see McGee and Gonza-léz 1999).

In Nahá today there are a few households with traditional women, that is, women whose husband's primary activity is making *milpa*. These women range in age from fifty to sixty or so years and their work revolves around the maintenance of the family and processing of food. They have little time to make marketable crafts. Additionally, since their families' main source of subsistence is the *milpa*, there is no need to spend much time on handicrafts, and little dependence on commercial income.

An example of a traditional family is Antonio Martinez and his wife Chan Nuk (#6), who is Chan K⁷in Viejo's eldest daughter by his second wife, Koh II. The family consists of Chan Nuk, Antonio, and their eleven children, four of whom still lived at home when the observations recorded here were conducted in 1996. Antonio cultivated three *milpas* and the family was among the few in Nahá who produced ample amounts of food in the summer of 1996.

Chan Nuk's day started at sunrise when she began grinding corn and shaping tortilla dough for the morning tortillas. She spent her day constantly involved in some aspect of food preparation. At any given time during the day Chan Nuk was involved in some aspect of the tortilla making. Luckily, much of the tortilla making process was compatible with other necessary household duties such as laundry, collecting firewood, and child care.

Chan Nuk also had four male children still in the household. Although sons are capable of performing domestic tasks, the Lacandon have traditionally designated domestic chores as women's work. Antonio and Chan Nuk's family still adhered to traditional gender roles. Just as Chan Nuk's sons did not participate in women's work, Chan Nuk did not perform traditional men's work, such as making *milpa*. The only acceptable men's work in which Chan Nuk participated was helping her husband assemble the arrows that he gave to his sons to sell for him.

# Women in Commercial Households

The move from subsistence farming to commercial activities has influenced indigenous people all over southern Mexico and Guatemala. Typically, Maya women have converted their domestic responsibilities, such as weaving or pottery making, into part-time commercial activities (Cancian 1987; Collier 1989; Ehlers 1990). In many cases, the shift from an agricultural to a wage-based economy among these Maya groups has caused a number of domestic changes that have had a negative impact on women. In an agricultural economy, a man and his wife have a reciprocal working relationship. The husband and wife see each other as equal contributors to their household's support. In the highland Maya community of Zinacantan, for example, maize is considered to be jointly owned by married couples (Flood, 1994:155). Men spend their days in the *milpa* working to produce food for their families. Women stay close to the home where they prepare meals, weave cloth, mend, and wash clothes, while keeping a watchful eye on their children. When households become increasingly dependent on cash income, the interdependent relationship between a woman and her husband tends to deteriorate. Food and clothing are bought in local markets, depreciating the value of a woman's labor. Unlike maize, wages are considered the property of the person who earns them. Consequently, with greater access to jobs outside the community, men typically earn larger amounts of money than women. As a result of their increased income, men enjoy a level of power and prestige not attainable by women. Additionally, unlike women who must divide their time between commercial activities and domestic tasks such as child care and food preparation, men are able to pursue commercial activities full-time. Thus, the commercial contribution a wife can make is less significant than the full-time efforts of her husband and this has led to the marginalization of women in some situations.

Interestingly, monetization among the Lacandon has not followed this pattern. Instead, Lacandon women have taken an active role in the tourist economy. They play a vital role in the production of tourist goods that are not continuations of their traditional domestic activities, and they typically control much of the profit generated by their work. Their activities in this new economy have opened up opportunities to expand their traditional roles and control their household's finances. I witnessed a clear and compelling example of the power that tourism has brought to some Northern Lacandon women in May 2001 when visiting Lacanha with a group of students from my university. In Lacanha, the group camped in a house compound composed of five households. These were led by an elder named Jorge; his three sons Enrique, K'in Panni Agua, and K'in Bol; and Vicente, K'in Bol's son-in-law. We hung hammocks and used tents in shelters provided by K'in Bol, while his wife Nuk prepared meals for the group using the foodstuffs we had brought with us from Palenque. When it came time to settle our account, Nuk showed us an itemized bill. When we pulled out our pesos to pay, K'in Bol asked if we would divide the bill into what we owed for lodging and what we owed for our meals. When I asked why, he explained that Nuk kept the money she earned preparing our meals and that he took only what we owed for the use of the shelter and tents. In that transaction, we paid Nuk the majority of the money.

I began my research with Lacandon women in the company of my wife, Stacie, and Belisa González, a student research assistant. The nontraditional wives in Nahá were the largest and youngest group of women we studied. The nontraditional wives we interviewed wore modern Mexican clothes and makeup while their husbands usually wore the *xikul*, the long, one-piece, white smock that is the hallmark of traditional male apparel. Men are typically the vendors of their crafts and have consciously maintained traditional dress as they believe it promotes an image that helps their craft sales. Women, who do not sell arts and crafts in public, do not promote this illusion. The few women who do sell handicrafts change into traditional attire during business hours.

Nontraditional wives spend their days engaged in many of the same activities as traditional wives. The women we spoke to washed clothes, watched children, and prepared food for their families. However, there were substantial differences in the implications of these activities. Because the husbands of nontraditional women were not full-time *milpa* farmers, the women's days did not revolve around the processing of corn. The bulk of their work, food preparation, had been substantially reduced by the purchase of products, such as canned food and a tortilla mix called *Maseca*. *Meseca* cuts tortilla-making time in half by eliminating several corn processing steps; there is no shelling, boiling, or grinding before the dough can be shaped into tortillas. Instead, women need only mix water with the mix, knead, shape, and cook the tortillas. Also, because *Maseca* dough has a lighter consistency, the women we observed used presses to shape the tortillas, which takes much less time than patting the tortillas out by hand. *Maseca*-made tortillas also cook faster because of their smaller, thinner size. All of the nontraditional women we spoke to supplemented their fresh corn dough with *Maseca* on a daily basis.

Several of the women admitted they were forced to use *Maseca* because the family had run out of their own corn. However, corn was readily available at local, state-run stores where prices of commodities are subsidized. In the summer of 1997, the price of corn was one peso per kilo which was well within the typical family's budget. We concluded that *Maseca* was popular because it was easy to use and provided women with extra time not enjoyed by traditional wives.

Because they are younger, most of these nontraditional wives also have dependent children, although their families are much smaller than families who have made a long-term investment in agriculture. Given fewer children to watch and time saved through the use of preprocessed foods, nontraditional wives have large blocks of time to help their husbands make bows and arrows and other marketable items. Nontraditional households thus generate much larger incomes than those households that invest time in agriculture, a fact that is reflected in the televisions, stereos, and manufactured goods found in their homes.

With their newfound free time, nontraditional wives have taken on new tasks. In particular, the nontraditional family's reliance on money generated by consumer goods and the pressure to produce large inventories for sale have allowed women to venture into the manufacture of goods, such as bows and arrows and incense burners, which are traditionally male items associated with male activities. Two of Chan K'in Viejo's older daughters, for example, became quite skilled at creating incense burners and clay animal figures. These women spent virtually every spare moment working on marketable crafts.

Not all nontraditional wives make clay figures, but all assist their husbands in making bow and arrow sets. In most cases, wives help their husbands assemble arrows by painting and attaching brightly colored chicken feathers to the arrow shafts and securing them with wax-coated string.

Another activity in which these nontraditional wives take part is handling the family finances. Unlike women in most Maya societies, the nontraditional women of Nahá in general, control their family's money. In fact, several husbands we spoke to admitted that they gave their wives the money they earned because if they kept the money it would be wasted on alcohol or other useless items. One man said that his wife took the money he earned so he would not *käxtik mehin bäk* (search for young game); in other words, so he would not spend it on other women. Generally among the families we interviewed, men turned the money they earned over to their wives. Although men might physically go to the store to buy items for the household, women kept the money and drew up the shopping lists. The television in Chan K'in Viejo's house, for example, was purchased at his wives' direction.

Kayum (#23) and his wife Chan Nuk Elisa provide a good example of a nontraditional couple who move back and forth between commerce and agriculture. In the summer of 1997, Kayum and Chan Nuk had an infant son and no *milpa;* instead, Kayum was stockpiling bow and arrow sets for the tourist season. I spent most of a day with them. After counting bows and arrows and questioning Kayum about the price of the pieces he was assembling, I started to take note of Chan Nuk's activities and the furnishings in their house. There was little furniture, just a bed, a table, and a set of chairs. There was also a baby walker and toys, and several large boxes of arrows. However, prominently displayed in the middle of the room was a color television that was left on the whole day. Chan Nuk had primary responsibility for their son (see Figure 4.3). Kayum concentrated almost exclusively on his arrows. When the baby slept Chan Nuk also assembled arrows. At midday she prepared a meal of tortillas made from a mix, pasta and tomatoes, and soft drinks. At the end of the day Kayum swept his work area, but he told me that Chan Nuk cleaned house, did laundry, and cooked. He also claimed that he gave the money he earned selling arrows to his wife. When I

**FIGURE 4.3**    Chan Nuk Elisa, 1997.

chided him about being lazy and not making a *milpa* he responded, "My work is making arrows."

What the example of Kayum and Chan Nuk demonstrates is that young Lacandon women can use their husband's commercial activities to expand their own roles and responsibilities. These new responsibilities, however, are added to the traditional roles they still play in their households, such as cooking and child care, and do not replace traditional tasks. Thus the new roles of young women keep them just as busy as their mothers who still spend most of their days grinding corn and cooking. Women in general have virtually no free time. Even when sitting in front of the television at the end of the day, women work at smaller tasks such as weaving baskets and net bags.

## Widows

The widows of Nahá are the oldest and in some ways the most interesting group. These women maintain their own independent households, cultivate their own *milpas*, and still manage to support dependent children with little help from their sons or other male relatives. When Chan K⁷in Viejo died in 1996, his two wives joined this group. Because of my increasing age and marriage, and with their husband's death, I have been able to cultivate a much closer relationship with the Kohs since 1996, and I have learned a lot about their lives. The Kohs have lived together for approximately thirty to thirty-five years. Between them they have borne over twenty children, five of whom still lived at home in 2001, ranging in age from nine to twenty years old. There are two girls, Chan Nuk and Chäx Nuk who are about seventeen and fourteen, and three boys, Chan K⁷in Sexto, age twenty , K⁷in, age seventeen, and the last, Chan K⁷in, who is eight years old. Chan K⁷in Sexto is old enough to make his own *milpa* and marry, but he chooses to remain in his mother's house. Even before Chan K⁷in Viejo's death at around age one hundred, the widows bore the brunt of the workload and depended only slightly on Chan K⁷in Sexto's help.

As they have for most of their lives, the Kohs are up early making tortillas and *ma⁷ats* for the morning meal. After the meal is finished, breakfast dishes washed, and a pot of shelled corn set on the fire, the women set off for one of their *milpas* with their daughters and youngest son. The widows spend at least every other day in one of their *milpas*, planting, weeding, and harvesting. Their husband was a tireless worker who used to cut and clear the *milpas* himself. Now, they hire men from the Tzeltal community of Lacandon to cut, clear, and burn their fields.

Typically arriving at their work site around nine in the morning, the two women begin to work, weeding, planting vegetables, harvesting fruits, and chopping wood. Chan K⁷in Sexto rarely helps and his younger brother K⁷in is excused because he attends school in the morning. Koh IV's younger daughter watches the eight-year-old who wanders around and entertains himself. The oldest daughter, Chan Nuk, generally works with the elder Koh or stays home to grind corn or do laundry. When the sun becomes hot the women quit their work and return home, where they immediately begin cooking the afternoon meal. After eating, they busy themselves with chores such as laundry and tending the chickens that they raise as a source of income. The women or one of their daughters also start shelling corn for the next day's tortillas and grinding dry corn to feed the chickens.

In addition to working in the *milpa,* doing laundry, supervising children, and caring for their poultry, the Kohs also collect firewood and tend their house gardens. They typically work cooperatively, with one woman starting a task and the other or one of the daughters completing it. It is because of this cooperation that the women have any time to fashion crafts. They make traditional clay figures, incense burners, net bags, and necklaces, which they give to their sons to sell for them or sell directly to visitors who occasionally come into the community. They also cultivate a large crop of tobacco which they dry and sell.

When I am in Nahá I rent a house from the Kohs and pay them for my meals. I also bring or buy corn, oatmeal, and other foodstuffs that I contribute to their kitchen. The income the Kohs earn from the sale of arts and crafts, chickens, eggs, vegetables, and tobacco is used to hire local Tzeltal to work in their *milpas,* at the cost of about 50 pesos per day. Even with this help, without the support of their sons or brothers, widows in Nahá such as the Kohs, are just one bad harvest away from starvation.

## Some Consequences of Tourism

### Diet

In many respects tourism has been a benefit to the Lacandon households with which I am familiar. However, there is another side to this story. As I have demonstrated, a part-time investment in the sale of crafts has little impact on food production at the household level. But a household's large-scale move to marketing goods to tourists is done at the expense of *milpa* agriculture and food production. Commercial enterprises typically lead to a decline in vegetable foods produced in Lacandon *milpas.* If *milpa* production decreases, it follows that there must be a corresponding increase in the purchase of prepackaged foods to supplement the decline in traditional crops.

When I lived in Chan K'in Viejo's compound during 1980 to 1983, the diet was primarily tortillas and beans supplemented by different fruits, such as bananas and oranges, vegetables, chicken eggs, and meat. A typical meal consisted of tortillas and beans seasoned with onions or cilantro, together with eggs or pasta shells cooked with tomatoes, and fruit. Once or twice a week meat was served—usually, chicken, fish, spider monkey, venison, or a rabbit-like rodent called *tepesquintli*. By 1995, however, the family diet had changed. Tortillas and beans were still the mainstay of a Lacandon meal. However, meals at which wild game is served—common during 1980 to 1983—are now rare. Men still hunt, but rarely find the deer, howler monkeys, and spider monkeys that were common in the forest a decade earlier. The increase in the Lacandon Jungle's population through immigration, and the resulting habitat destruction, have virtually eliminated these resources around Nahá.

Today, the Lacandon supplement their diets with chicken, beef, fish, and fruit purchased from traveling vendors. Many families also have to buy corn from stores in local communities because they have not planted a *milpa* or do not grow enough to feed themselves. In 1995, a variety of packaged foods were also served. Some of these, served during February and March of 1995, are listed here:

| | | |
|---|---|---|
| cheese | canned tuna | canned peppers |
| pasta | canned ham | herbal tea |
| rice | dried fish | Nestlé's Quik |
| instant coffee | beef | soft drinks |
| popcorn | canned sardines | sugar |
| bouillon cubes | powdered milk | oatmeal |

Families now buy products that they formerly produced themselves, such as fish, popcorn, and chili peppers. Additionally, they have substituted many items in the traditional, largely vegetarian, diet for items that are much higher in fat and sugar content such as soft drinks, canned fish, chocolate powdered milk, and cheese.

The impact of these dietary changes on the health and physical well-being of Lacandon families has yet to be measured. My preliminary (and admittedly unscientific) observation is that the Lacandon families who rely most on store-bought rather than *milpa*-produced foods are heavier and have poorer dental health than the families that focus on *milpa* farming and adhere more closely to the traditional vegetarian diet. Additionally, processed foods are an added expense to a family's budget and compel them to make an even greater effort to sell tourist goods. In the short term, if your family is running out of food you need money to buy food. You do not have the time to plant a *milpa* and wait for the harvest.

## Commerce, Reciprocity, and Status

The community of Nahá is composed of a number of compounds, each comprising several households of extended families. While the individual family is the the basic unit of food production and consumption, reciprocity is practiced within the house compound. In Chan K'in Viejo's compound, the Kohs' kitchen is the center of activity as a constant stream of daughters and, to a lesser degree, sons stop by to visit and exchange supplies throughout the day.

Reciprocity is an economic feature of many horticultural societies. It typically structures the distribution of resources and may serve as a mechanism to reinforce egalitarianism. Reciprocity between households within a compound is an essential feature of the traditional Lacandon subsistence economy. Women freely exchange produce from *milpas* and gardens, eggs, and fruit between members of related households. To a degree, household labor, such as gathering firewood or supervising children, is also exchanged. In the Kohs' kitchen, a typical exchange might involve bunches of onions for eggs, or tomatoes for oranges. Anyone walking into a house where food is being prepared is instantly offered a seat at the table. Men share their labor and the meat from the game they kill with the other households in the compound. Related men will also work together to make *milpa* for the family of a man who is unable to do so himself. For example, in 1997 Kayum (#23), although not making a *milpa* for himself, helped tend the fields of the son of one of his older brothers. This second young man was being held in the Ocosingo jail during the crucial planting months of the spring, and his uncles tended his *milpa* until his release. In a subsistence economy where the raw materials of household subsistence are freely available to all, this type of reciprocity reinforces social networks and provides a form of insurance in case of localized crop failures or other environmental hazards.

However, the goal in a commercial economy is profit, not subsistence. At Palenque, Lacandon families compete against each other for the attention of tourists—and in a competitive system, when one side wins the other side loses. Some men are assertive promoters of their crafts, shouting over their companions or aggressively approaching groups of potential customers. These individuals sell many more items than their more reserved comrades and their homes are lavishly equipped with manufactured goods. In 1980, a Lacandon home considered wealthy had a tin roof or a cement slab floor but the traditional two-room house plan was shared by all members of the community. A wealthy family had a battery-operated radio or tape player, and some plastic bowls and cups instead of the traditional gourd utensils. Chairs, tables, and other furnishings were handmade. Today, differences of material wealth between households are dramatic. Some successful vendors have built multiroom homes equipped with store-bought furniture. Since the introduction of electricity to the community in 1993, many houses are equipped with televisions and stereo equipment almost as elaborate as that in any middle-class North American home.

The money earned in the tourist trade and the consumer goods purchased by successful vendors are not products that can be shared according to the traditional rules of house compound reciprocity. A television costing hundreds of dollars cannot be exchanged for bunches of onions or a bag of oranges, or borrowed for a morning's work. Lacandon I have discussed this issue with are acutely aware that there are now haves and have-nots in their community. Some men and women are jealous of those who have acquired material success, and feel that the old rules of reciprocity are not followed by younger men and women. Immersion in the crafts trade appears to have encouraged the accumulation of private household goods that cannot be shared according to the traditional pattern. This differential access to consumer goods, and the lack of sharing of these items between households, may ultimately provide the basis for the stratification of Lacandon society. Such a process is described by Collier (1989, 1994) for Maya Indians in the highlands of Chiapas. In communities within the *municipio* of Zinacantan, Collier shows how opportunities for wage labor, the decline in subsistence agriculture, and increasing reliance on money have led to increasing internal stratification and widening disparities in Zinacanteco standards of living.

The decline of reciprocal relationships discussed here refers specifically to relations among young men and women, and the commercially produced manufactured products they have acquired. Men and women whose tasks revolve principally around *milpa*, house gardens, child care, household maintenance, and food preparation, continue to participate in multigenerational reciprocal relationships between households. At the household level, this typically takes the form of keeping an eye on each other's children and sharing locally produced food, such as eggs, vegetables, and fruits.

The resentment that some older men have expressed to me concerning the material success of younger individuals also indicates that traditional forms of prestige and authority are being challenged. Before the Lacandon's large-scale entry into the tourist industry, the elderly were respected because of their age and accumulated wisdom. Chan K'in Viejo's position in Nahá is a classic example. In 1980, he was a patriarch of the community, respected for his ritual knowledge, age, and experience. He was active in community affairs and his opinion was respected at community meetings. When the community's location changed in the summer of 1979, for example, it was Chan K'in Viejo who led the move. By the time of his death in December 1996, he was a beloved but marginalized figure in the community. Tourists came to literally sit at his feet, but he was no longer consulted on community decisions and the religious rituals he treasured had largely been abandoned by the men in the community, including his sons. What happened was that in the decade prior to his death a competing model of status was introduced into the community. In previous generations, prestigious men were those who had bountiful *milpas*, multiple wives, and large families. Today, younger men enhance their prestige through their success in the sale of goods to tourists and the accompanying acquisition of material goods. Even Chan K'in Viejo's eldest sons have not followed his path. Chan K'in (#8) operates the main store in town. Though he practices some rituals privately in his father's god house, he no longer bothers with a *milpa*. K'in (#9) and Chan K'in Tercero (#10) have moved to Palenque permanently and are making a living selling bows and arrows. Even worse for elderly men, this new form of status represents a type of achievement that is denied those who are unwilling or unable to compete with their neighbors in the tourist trade.

The social and economic changes that the Lacandon are experiencing sound remarkably similar to the social and political transformations described by Collier (1989) and Cancian (1987) for the Zinacantecan Maya in the Chiapas highlands, and these may serve as a model for the future of Lacandon society. According to Cancian (1987:134–136), who studied men in the hamlet of Nachig, the shift from subsistence farming to wage labor created a shift in economic and political leadership in Zinacantecan hamlets. In the 1960s, only older corn farming men in Nachig had high rank. Two decades later, with 62 percent of young men working for wages rather than subsistence farming, age was no longer correlated with economic or political rank.

The Lacandon case is slightly different in that Lacandon are merchants who sell their own crafts rather than individuals who sell their labor. However, economic stratification of Lacandon society by material wealth is now a fact in Nahá. Although still egalitarian in their social relations, if the Lacandon follow the Zinacanteco pattern, differences in material wealth may ultimately lead to differential access to political power and social influence within the community.

In addition to the Lacandon elders' loss of status, the monetary success of younger men has altered the relations of work in Lacandon society. The incomes of some young men have liberated them from the control traditionally exercised by their fathers and fathers-in-law. As described at the start of this chapter, young men formerly worked for their fathers until they celebrated the *hetzmek* that ushered them into adult manhood. After marrying they worked in the service of their fathers-in-law. However, this rite of passage has been abandoned. The last celebration of the *hetzmek* of which I am aware occurred just after the completion of the Palenque road in 1980.

Marriage is still a marker of adulthood in Lacandon society, but most young men prefer to pay bride wealth and avoid the years of servitude to their fathers-in-law. Recently, one young man in Nahá married a young woman from Lacanha. A few months into his bride service, he and his wife returned to Nahá for a visit but never returned to Lacanha. The young man never fulfilled his work obligation. Instead he sent his father-in-law money. Two other young men have even married *ladina* girls from Palenque, thus avoiding bride price altogether. Additionally, successful Lacandon vendors no longer need an extended family's help to build a household and make a *milpa*. They can afford to buy the materials they need and hire Tzeltal Maya to do their *milpa* work.

This process is not unique to the Lacandon. Collier (1989:119) has similarly demonstrated a relationship between the increase in wage labor in Zinacantan, and the decline in traditional courting rituals and the payment of bride wealth. In the hamlet of Apas, wage work has freed Zinacanteco youths from economic dependence on their elders, which had been reinforced by traditional marriage customs and the bride wealth system.

Demographic changes have also accompanied the economic shifts in Nahá since 1980. The elder men of Nahá, such as Chan K'in Viejo, Matejo Viejo, and Antonio had dozens of children to help in their households. As their sons married, they had sons-in-law performing bride service who replaced the loss of their sons' labor. Even today, if a young man pays bride wealth instead of working for his father-in-law, the older man can hire Tzeltal Maya to work in his *milpas*. However, this situation may be more severe for men of the next generation. Middle-aged families in Nahá today typically have three to five children. Table 4.7 provides a

**TABLE 4.7   Number of Children per Family by Generation**

| Age | 20–30 | 30–40 | 40–50 | 60+ |
|---|---|---|---|---|
| Family 1 | 2 | 3 | 7 | 10 |
| Family 2 | 2 | 4 | 6 | 10 |
| Family 3 | 1 | 4 | 4 | 9 |
| Family 4 | 2 | 3 | 2 | |
| Family 5 | 1 | 3 | 5 | |
| Family 6 | 1 | 2 | 5 | |
| Family 7 | 2 | 3 | 3 | |
| Family 8 | 1 | | | |
| Family 9 | 3 | | | |
| Family 10 | 1 | | | |
| Average Size | 1.6 | 3.1 | 4.5 | 9.6 |

sample of twenty-seven Lacandon households divided by generation, and clearly shows that family size is decreasing. Of course,
younger couples have had less time to have children than middle-aged couples, but birth control techniques are known and
used by the younger women in Nahá and the women I talked to
typically said they wanted no more than two children.

As their sons grow and leave to start their own families,
middle-aged men with only one or two children will not have
sons-in-law to replace this loss of labor. Because rights to labor
through kinship are being replaced by contractual relations based
on the payment of wages, households are even more dependent
on incomes generated by tourism. Consequently, as they age, men
without incomes or with few children will be unable to support
themselves through traditional agricultural means and will not
have sons-in-law to help support their households.

Formerly, elders who were unable to support themselves
could rely on the support of their children to survive. In an economy based on subsistence agriculture where children work and
one person can grow enough food for many, supporting nonpro-
ductive family members is not a great burden on the members of
a household. Support of the elderly in a market economy, where
incomes are limited and dependent on a steady supply of tourists,
is inherently less secure.

Agriculture and commerce have developed an uneasy coex-
istence in Nahá today. When families adopt a commercial existence at the expense of the traditional agricultural lifestyle the
result can be the straining of reciprocal social relationships and
increasing dependence on economic forces far beyond a household's control. At the same time, traditional religion, which could
have been a central unifying force, has been abandoned.

The Lacandon are successful merchants. However, the
worst-case view of their commercial success, I am afraid, may be
measured in eroded fields and declining yields. If their market
economy continues to expand, the economic polarization of Lacandon households will become more pronounced. Traditional
patterns of subsistence and reciprocity may completely give way
to profit-oriented behavior between competing households.

As new immigrants continue to cut down the forest and the
Lacandon population grows, agriculture and the populations of
game animals will continue to decline, forcing Lacandon families

to expand their efforts to sell tourist goods or start cash cropping beans and chilies like their neighbors. In the near future, I believe the forces that now push them toward a commercial economy will continue to build. However, commercial success carries a price. So far most Lacandon men and women seem to be able to successfully balance their subsistence strategies between agriculture and tourism. In the following section I present the case studies of two young Lacandon men who grew up during these last two turbulent decades. One has made a very successful life in the new Lacandon economy. The second maintained a more traditional life but was ultimately a victim of a crime at the hands of one of his companions.

## Growing Up in a Changing World: The Cases of K'in and Chan K'in Quinto

In 1980, there were seven children in Chan K'in Viejo's household. These were, in order of age: K'in, the last child of Koh III, and Chan Nuk, Chan K'in Quinto, Nuk, Kayum, Bol, and Chan K'in Sexto (born in 1981), the children of Koh IV. Of these seven children I knew the eldest, K'in (#18), the best because we shared quarters during my first years in Nahá. Although most Lacandon would probably tell you that a good son works with his father in the *milpa*, I have rarely seen teenage boys do much work and K'in was no exception. Koh IV's sons Chan K'in Quinto and Kayum, approximately eight and six, spent much more time helping their mother and father than K'in. This is not to say that K'in was exceptionally lazy. He regularly cut firewood and was his father's main ritual assistant in the god house. If there were copal incense trees to tap, incense boards to prepare, or *balché* drinking gourds to wash K'in was there to help. In 1981 and 1982, he also took the time to help me transcribe and translate tapes of his father's stories.

K'in provided my introduction to the bows and arrows industry that had sprung up to meet the rising tourist demand in Palenque. K'in and one of his buddies, a son of Matejo Viejo, spent a great deal of time making bundles of bows and arrows that his older brothers took to Palenque and sold for him. For example, in October of 1981 K'in had made a bundle of three hundred arrows and by that December he had earned almost $400 U.S. In fact, the bows and arrows are probably the reason K'in did little *milpa* work.

**FIGURE 4.4**   K'in, 1981.

As a young man in his mid-teens (see Figure 4.4) K'in was old enough to strike out on his own, make his own *milpa*, and look for a wife. Making a *milpa* was a prerequisite for marriage in generations past. However, K'in was one of the first young men that I saw take a different path. Rather than make *milpa*, K'in spent most of his time making bows and arrows and gave part of the proceeds of the sale of his crafts to his father. In that way he still contributed to his family's support, even though he rarely spent time in a *milpa*. At the same time, he saved money toward his future marriage.

K'in was interested in marriage by 1981, and that year he complained a lot about the lack of available women in Nahá. In Palenque that fall, he trimmed his hair and bought pants and a shirt to wear on the street because he thought it made him look more attractive to the young women there. In the summer of 1983,

K'in married Maria, a Tzeltal Maya woman from the nearby community of Lacandon. He performed his bride service there, then moved his wife and family back to Nahá. Today he has four children.

In 1993, K'in started a small store in Nahá selling snacks, soap, candles, and similar household necessities. An astute businessman, he established a branch store adjacent to a nearby army base that was established in the spring of 1995 at the outset of the Zapatista rebellion. This has been a profitable endeavor in that he has established friendly ties with the soldiers as well as a successful business. When his house and store burned to the ground in June of 1999, a squad of soldiers arrived the next day to clean up the site and help him rebuild.

One of the most interesting aspects of K'in's life is that when he married he converted to Christianity and began attending an evangelical Presbyterian church in the town of Lacandon. In 1995, he built a small one-room temple on the grounds of his house compound where he hosts occasional services that are led by a visiting lay minister from Lacandon.

Happily, I have found no evidence of tension between non-Christians and Christians in Nahá. I feared conflict because I had seen some of the hard feelings that were created in Mensäbäk between those Lacandon who converted to Seventh Day Adventism in the late 1970s and those who did not. The attitude in Nahá seems to be live and let live. K'in and his wife do not push their views on their friends or family, and his family does not judge K'in for his beliefs. The one time I talked to K'in's father about the conversion of Lacandons to Christianity in 1995, Chan K'in Viejo said that he thought that conversion to Christianity was all right because the converts stopped drinking and beating their wives and children.

Unfortunately, alcohol and the money to purchase it has been an unhappy combination in Nahá. Several young men have died in alcohol-related accidents. Numerous young men have been assaulted in Palenque and San Cristobal after drinking bouts, and several marriages have ended because young husbands became abusive with their wives or children after drinking binges.

The story of Chan K'in Quinto, my young *milpa* guide and translator is tied to alcohol. In 1983, Quinto became my roommate when his older brother K'in married and moved to the town of

Lacandon. I worked with him in his father's *milpa* and watched as his father taught him how to make incense boards and pray in front of the god pots. I paid him small amounts to guide me on walks through the forest and teach me Lacandon vocabulary. In particular, I remember a trick he played that gave me the opportunity to witness firsthand a rare display of Lacandon anger.

Nahá has been in its current location on the eastern side of a small lake since 1979 and 1980. One sunny afternoon in April 1981, I took a walk with Quinto to visit the old Nahá on the north shore of the lake. The old site was largely overgrown but well-marked by the groves of orange trees planted around the decaying houses. At the time, I did not know that the person who plants a fruit tree continues to own the fruit even if he no longer resides on the land. Chan K'in Quinto led me straight to a large stand of trees loaded with fruit, climbed into a tree and began throwing oranges down, which I dutifully collected in the bags I had brought. When the bags were full, I thought it strange that Quinto started to stuff himself with oranges and ate a bagful during our walk back to the village. I wondered what his hurry was. In my happy ignorance I marched into the kitchen, tossed my bags of oranges on the table and announced that I had brought oranges for everyone. Then Koh asked Quinto where I had picked the oranges. There was a rapid exchange that I could not follow, and then Quinto disappeared. A few minutes later an angry Matejo Viejo called on me and gave me a piece of his mind. Quinto had led me to Matejo's trees and without permission I had collected his oranges.

In many ways, Quinto was less modern than his older brother K'in. He did not spend much time making bows and arrows, preferring to work in his *milpa*. He married a women from Nahá in 1988, and for a while he and his wife shared quarters with me in Chan K'in Viejo's unmarried son's quarters. I stayed out of their way, they ignored me, and when I returned the following year they had moved. Then Quinto disappeared from my field notes. I rarely saw him, and he did not visit me on my return trips to Nahá. Others told me that he was mean and to be avoided when he drank too much. When I ran in to him it was when he was visiting his father. In the spring of 1995, he was one of the most frequent visitors to his father's house and he was always polite to me. Although I knew where he lived, I never visited him and he did not seek my company. In the winter of 1999, I heard that he and his wife had a baby.

In the spring of 1999, I was shocked to hear that he had been found bludgeoned to death after a night of drinking with some Lacandon companions. Although speculation was rampant, no one in Nahá admits to having witnessed the crime. Two young men from Nahá were suspected but, after an investigation turned up no conclusive evidence, they were released from jail in Ocosingo and returned home to a community deeply divided over the question of their guilt. His wife, left destitute after Quinto's death, moved back to her mother's house with her baby.

# CHAPTER

# 5 The Decline of Traditional Religious Practices in Nahá

I initially chose to work with the Lacandon in Nahá because they were not Christian. For a decade and a half I studied their rites, mythology, and ritual symbolism, and I traced the links between ancient Maya and contemporary Lacandon religion. Today only three individuals in Nahá continue to practice the traditional rituals with any regularity. Although tourism oriented to the Lacandon continues to focus on religion, the religious complex in which I participated in the 1980s, organized around agricultural and healing rituals, the sacred mead *balché,* and symbols of human sacrifice, has been abandoned. The pantheon of gods in the forest and sky, whose benevolence and protection was ensured through offerings of food and incense have been discarded. Ritual huts have fallen into disrepair leaving incense burners, the portals between this world and the supernatural, exposed to the elements. Non-Christian rituals have become another money-making opportunity carried out for tourists and filmmakers. Unlike the people in Mensäbäk and Lacanha, the people of Nahá have not converted to Christianity. Most men have simply ceased to perform religious rituals of any kind. In this chapter I take a brief look at Lacandon religion as I watched it practiced in the early 1980s and trace its disappearance as young men shifted away from the traditional farming economy. In Chapter 6, I discuss religious healing rites that have been replaced by Western medical technology.

**TABLE 5.1    Some Lacandon Deities**

| God | Relationship | Responsibilities |
| --- | --- | --- |
| K?akoch | | Creator of gods |
| Hachäkyum | | Creator of humans |
| Sukunkyum | Hachäkyum's older brother | Lord of the underworld; judges souls |
| Äkyantho? | Hachäkyum's older brother | Lord of foreigners |
| Kisin | Hachäkyum's brother-in-law | Lord of Death |
| T?uup | Hachäkyum's son | Carries sun in the sky |
| Äk?inchob | Hachäkyum's son-in-law | Lord of the *milpa* |
| Mensäbäk | | Lord of rain |
| Känänk?ax | | Guardian of the forest; protector of *milperos* |
| Itsanal | | Hachäkyum's assistant |

# Cosmology

The ritual activity described in my book *Life, Ritual, and Religion among the Lacandon Maya* (1990) was acted out in a cosmological context that is shared by most Maya groups and has its roots in the belief system of the ancient Maya. The men I worked with in 1980 believed that we lived in a multilayered cosmos. The creator of the gods and the world was the god K?akoch. He lived in the uppermost layer of the cosmos, remote and uninterested in human affairs. K?akoch created the gods to worship him, which they did in the same manner that the Lacandon worshiped K?akoch's creations. The deities that K?akoch created came into being when they emerged from the *bäk nikte*, or plumeria flower. Some of the principal deities are listed in Table 5.1.

| God | Relationship | Responsibilities |
| --- | --- | --- |
| Itsanok²uh | | Hachäkyum's assistant |
| K²ulel | | Hachäkyum's assistant; sweeps his house |
| Säkäpuk | | Hachäkyum's assistant |
| Tsibatnah | Mensäbäk's younger brother | Paints gods' homes at Yaxchilan with human blood |
| Bol | | Maker of *balché* |
| Kayum | | Sings to gods during their *balché* rituals |
| Xkale²ox | | Name of all gods' wives |
| Äk Nah | | "Our Mother," the moon goddess |
| U nail | | "Wife of" title, given to all gods' wives |

K²akoch created the earth as a formless mass. When Hachä-kyum (the creator of humans) stepped down from the plumeria flower he was dissatisfied with what he saw and threw sand down onto the ground to give the world form. He then separated the layers of the cosmos. Hachäkyum raised the sky like "smoke rising into the air," according to Chan K²in Viejo. He then placed the sun and moon in a layer of the cosmos under K²akoch, where they were carried through the sky by Hachäkyum's son T²uup. Hachäkyum then created his own layer of sky, *u ka²ani Hachäkyum*, which is the layer of sky where the celestial deities reside. Below that is *u ka²ani chom*, the "vulture's sky" in which are found the clouds and the sky humans see. Humans live on the surface or *lu²um*. Beneath us is the *yalam lu²um*, or underworld, that is in-habited by Sukunkyum and Kisin (see Figure 5.1).

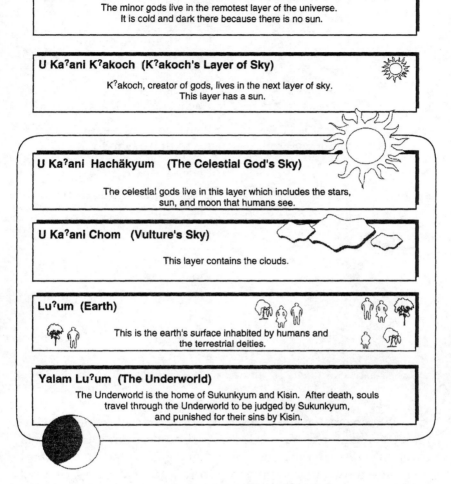

**U Kaʔani Chembel Kʔuh  (The Minor God's Sky)**

The minor gods live in the remotest layer of the universe.
It is cold and dark there because there is no sun.

**U Kaʔani Kʔakoch  (Kʔakoch's Layer of Sky)**

Kʔakoch, creator of gods, lives in the next layer of sky.
This layer has a sun.

**U Kaʔani Hachäkyum    (The Celestial God's Sky)**

The celestial gods live in this layer which includes the stars,
sun, and moon that humans see.

**U Kaʔani Chom   (Vulture's Sky)**

This layer contains the clouds.

**Luʔum  (Earth)**

This is the earth's surface inhabited by humans and
the terrestrial deities.

**Yalam Luʔum  (The Underworld)**

The Underworld is the home of Sukunkyum and Kisin.  After death, souls
travel through the Underworld to be judged by Sukunkyum,
and punished for their sins by Kisin.

**FIGURE 5.1**   The cosmos according to Chan Kʔin Viejo.

Sukunkyum is the lord of the underworld. Kisin causes death. When humans die their *pixan,* or souls, make a three-day journey through the underworld where they must face Sukunkyum. He stares into their eyes, reviews their conduct, and either sends the souls back to the surface to spend the afterlife in the house of the rain god Mensäbäk, or gives the souls to Kisin who destroys them or turns them into his draft animals. Kisin, who Chan Kʔin Viejo described as fair-skinned, mustached, and wearing a hat (like the Guatemalan Maximon), also causes earthquakes by kicking the large stone pillars in the underworld that hold up the surface world on which we live.

## Ritual Places

### Classic Period Ruins

Before the secularization of their society, the ritual activity of Lacandon men was conducted in three areas: Classic Period ruins, cave shrines and rock shelters, and a family's god house.

Lacandon incense burners have been discovered at a variety of archeological sites between the Jatate, Pasión, and Usumacinta Rivers. Thompson (1977) reports on Lacandon incense burners found at the site of Piedras Negras in the 1930s. Fifty years earlier, Maler (1903) reported finding Lacandon *incensarios* at El Cayo and Yaxchilan. Lacandon ritual paraphernalia has also been encountered at Bonampak which is near the community of Lacanha.

The ruins of Yaxchilan and to a lesser degree Palenque at one time occupied a special place in the religious beliefs of the men in Nahá. Palenque today is a commercially important site, for it draws the tourists to whom the majority of Lacandon market their crafts. However, according to Chan K'in Viejo, Palenque was the original home of the gods in the initial period of creation when Hachäkyum was fashioning the earth's surface, making humans, and creating the underworld for his brother Sukunkyum. According to Chan K'in Viejo, Hachäkyum and his wife made human beings from sand and kernels of corn in the north court of the *Palacio* at Palenque. Once when visiting the ruins with two of Chan K'in Viejo's sons, I was told that the larger-than-life-sized carvings of captives in the north courtyard of the *Palacio* are representations of these original creations.

Chan K'in Viejo also identified the *axis mundi* of their cosmos as a ceiba tree that formerly grew in the courtyard where humans were created. Bruce and Torrijos (1991) reference a Lacandon myth that tells of a giant ceiba tree in the courtyard of the *Palacio* whose branches reached the sky and roots penetrated into the underworld. Like the ancient Maya, the Lacandon associate the Milky Way with this giant ceiba/*axis mundi*. In the Lacandon language the Milky Way is called *säk bel äkyum*, "white road of our lords." Like the ancient Maya, Chan K'in Viejo said the gods used this road to travel back and forth between this world and the sky.

Several men told me that the stars are light we see shining through the holes poked in our sky by roots of trees growing in Hachäkyum's forest. Thus one of the Lacandon names for the stars is *mots che,* meaning "tree roots."

Despite the cosmology associated with Palenque, there is no historical or archeological evidence that Palenque has ever been an important site for Lacandon pilgrims. This is probably because the Lacandon gods do not live there. One Lacandon myth describes how the gods who built Palenque came to abandon it in favor of Yaxchilan. The myth tells how Hachäkyum fashioned a surrogate made of palm leaves to take his place while he was away making the underworld (Bruce 1974:154–169). Jealous of their father's power, two of Hachäkyum's sons, Paal äkyum Chäk Xib and Kʔakʔ Bäkʔel äkyum Chäk Xib, shot the surrogate full of arrows thinking it was their father. When Hachäkyum returned and saw what his sons had done he banished them to Palenque and moved to Yaxchilan. Yaxchilan is the site of most of the events described in the mythology of the people of Nahá. One exception is the rain god Mensäbäk who is associated with the Ocosingo Valley and the site of Toniná.

Yaxchilan is a three-day walk almost directly east of Nahá. It wasn't until 1995, when I made a pilgrimage to Yaxchilan with a Lacandon elder (who asked to remain anonymous), that I learned that Yaxchilan's orientation to Nahá is the reason the entrance to Lacandon god houses and god pots always faces the east. On the first day of the pilgrimage I was given a Lacandon tour of the Grand Plaza. Most visitors to Yaxchilan enter the site through Structure 19, called the Labyrinth because you must wind your way through a short maze of passages (see Map 5.1). This structure was built in the middle of the seventh century C.E., during the reign of Bird Jaguar III, and its entrance is aligned with the winter solstice sunrise. For the Lacandon, this is the house of Itsanal, one of Hachäkyum's assistants. This was the first spot where my companions burned copal incense. We know Lacandon pilgrims were leaving offerings in this structure before 1900 because Teobert Maler found Lacandon incense burners there during his explorations of the ruins in the 1890s. Structure 78, at the north end of the Labyrinth complex, is Itsanal's kitchen.

After passing through the Labyrinth, we entered the Grand Plaza. The ball court is located on the north side of the plaza, but the Lacandon today know nothing of the ancient ball game.

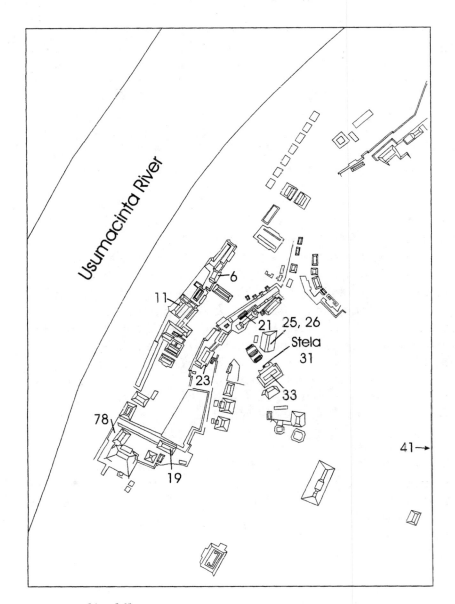

**MAP 5.1   Yaxchilan.**

Across from the ball court on the south side of the plaza is Structure 23. Structure 23 is well known because it once housed the Lintels 24 and 25 that depicted Shield Jaguar and his consort Lady Xok. In Lintel 24, Lady Xok is pictured conducting a bloodletting rite in which she draws a cord with thorns through her tongue.

Unfortunately, these lintels were removed and shipped to England in 1882 and 1883 by the English explorer Alfred Maudsley. Contemporary Lacandon have no knowledge of them. To my Lacandon guide, Structure 23 was simply the house of Bol, the Lacandon god who makes the sacred mead *balché*. Just to the north of Bol's house is Structure 11, the house of the sun god K'in.

Walking east down the plaza we next visited Structure 6 which is best known for the stucco frieze on the building's southern facade. Maler (1903) found Lacandon incense burners there during his 1895 exploration of the structure, and later archeologists also reported finding large numbers of Lacandon ceramics and other offerings during their excavations in the 1980s (García Moll and Cossío 1986). My Lacandon friends identified the stucco mask on Structure 6 as the god Säkäpuk. The lower part of the building is his house. The upper roof comb of Structure 6 is the home of Äk'inchob, the Maize Kernel Priest, who is the Lacandon lord of the *milpa* and guards humans from harm in the forest. Maler (1903:125) called Structure 6 the "Red Temple" because the exterior at one time had been painted bright red. The north side of Structure 6, a shallow room with three wide doorways, is the site where, according to Lacandon myth, Hachäkyum assembled the Lacandon, slit their throats, and used the blood to paint his home. We do not know the activities that were conducted in Structure 6 during its original occupation. However, it is obvious that the Lacandon associated their myth with this building because of its red color. Similarly, Lacandon men painted red designs on beams of their god houses in imitation of the blood used to decorate the gods' homes at Yaxchilan. Finally, Structure 21 is the house of Kayum, another of Hachäkyum's assistants, who plays and sings during the gods' *balché* rites.

On the second day of our pilgrimage, we went up into the ruins soon after sunrise for the Lacandon men to make their offerings. Before entering the site through the Labyrinth, we stopped to wash our hands and my guides changed into clean smocks. The elder of the two also stopped to pick *xate*, palm leaves, with which to make ceremonial wands. We then proceeded directly to the base of Structure 33, the great pyramid built during the reign of Bird Jaguar IV (752–771). For the Lacandon, Structure 33 is the home of Hachäkyum. It is the most important ritual spot in the entire site for the Lacandon, and different families have probably been making pilgrimages to this spot for a couple of centuries. Alfred Maudsley camped in Structure 33 when he visited Yaxchilan in 1882, and reported finding large numbers of Lacandon incense burners deposited in the temple.

As we ascended the Grand Stairway of Structure 33 we passed Structures 25 and 26, which my guides identified as Hachäkyum's kitchens. Just below the summit of the pyramid is a small plaza in the center of which is Stela 31, a stalactite. My guides described the stalactite as the *che tuch lu'um*, meaning "tree-earth umbilicus." They identified this spot as the center point from which the earth was made and where the earth had been connected to the sky. Chan K'in Viejo later described this spot as the *"koben Hachäkyum,"* or Hachäkyum's hearth. He said that long ago they used to dance and sing to Hachäkyum around this monument. Maler mentions hearing a similar story during one of his visits to the site (1903:162).

The temple at the top of the Grand Stairway of Structure 33 has three doors and several interior chambers. On the riser in front of the building's entrance are scenes of ballplayers, which the men accompanying me identified as men watching the moon. In the center chamber, facing the middle door, is a headless statue of a seated Bird Jaguar IV. This figure is the focus of most Lacandon offerings at the site. Lacandon call this statue the *Hach Bilaan Hachäkyum,* and say it is a representation of the deity who created them. According to Lacandon mythology, Hachäkyum has ordered the destruction of humans three times. Offerings are made in front of the statue to forestall his destruction of this era of creation.

Tate (1989, 1992) presents convincing evidence that many of the structures at Yaxchilan were built with an orientation to the summer and winter solstices. This plan is most obvious with Structure 33 (see Figure 5.2). Bird Jaguar IV constructed the pyramid as a monument to his reign and aligned the structure so that it would mark the summer solstice sunrise by illuminating his statue at the summit of the pyramid. Like their Classic Period counterparts, the Lacandon continue to believe that Structure 33 has a relationship with the sun, although they do not systematically track the sun's movement or mark the solstices. Men of Nahá view this building as a model of the upper levels of the cosmos, with the frieze and roof comb representing different layers of the

**FIGURE 5.2**    Temple 33 at Yaxchilan.

sky. The building itself is Hachäkyum's home on the earth while the elaborate frieze represents Hachäkyum's layer of sky. The roof comb represents the level of sky inhabited by Hachäkyum's son T?uup, whose job it is to carry the sun through the sky. The large stucco figure at the center of the roof comb is a representation of T?uup, according to Chan K?in Viejo. Curiously, even though the Lacandon in Nahá pay no particular attention to the exact dates of the solstices, their concept of Structure 33 maintains the solar association intended by its builders.

In traditional Lacandon religion there are a variety of offerings that simulate human sacrifice and bloodletting. They are a mild imitation of the sacrificial rituals of their ancestors. On this day, after praying in front of the statue of Hachäkyum, the Lacandon men prepared offerings of a *xikal*, or incense board, and humanoid rubber figures called *k?ik?*. Both offerings are meant to replicate human beings and, as the offerings were held out for Hachäkyum's approval, the elder man in our group recited a prayer to ensoul and animate the offerings before they were burned.

The offering ceremonies were concluded by 11 in the morning and we left the site, stopping only at Structure 19 to burn two more *xikal* offerings to Itsanal. Once we had exited through the Labyrinth, the men changed back into their everyday smocks and we proceeded back to the campsite. In passing, my Lacandon guides mentioned that the larger pyramid located behind Hachäkyum's house, Structure 41, was the house of the god K²ulel. K²ulel assists Hachäkyum and sweeps his house and god house. Like Structure 33, Structure 41 is aligned to mark the summer solstice sunrise.

## Caves and Rock Shelters

Another location for offering rites to traditional Lacandon gods are cave shrines and rock shelters (see Figure 5.3). These sites, typically homes of terrestrial deities, were popular destinations for pilgrims who would bring offerings of god pots and burn copal incense. In 1980, for example, I visited the cave shrine visited by Maler on the day of his first face-to-face encounter with a Lacandon in September 1898 (described in Chapter 1). The shrine is dedicated to the god Ah K²ak² who was feared for the sickness he caused. He received many offerings to placate his wrath. When

**FIGURE 5.3**  Rock shelter shrine near Mensäbäk, 1980.

I visited the shrine, the area under the rock overhang was strewn with hundreds of god pots and bowls of incense and also contained the skeletal remains of at least three people. Interestingly, the foreheads of the skulls were flattened in the manner of the pre-Hispanic Maya, although how long the bones have been in the shelter is impossible to say. Unfortunately, I have seen recent photographs of these remains, taken by visitors in Mensäbäk, that shows that they have deteriorated badly in the years since I visited the shrine.

In 1996, I had the opportunity to visit another type of cave shrine. In this cave old god pots were discarded after the incense burner renewal ceremony. God pots are believed to be living beings and the most important part of the incense burner renewal ceremony is painting and ensouling the new god pots and killing the old. The ancient Maya ritually killed implements by breaking them. The Lacandon, however, kill their god pots by removing the stone and cacao beans in the bowl of the incense burner and burning the paint off them. The cacao beans represent the burner's internal organs and the stone is the seat on which the gods rest when attending a ceremony. The paint is the garment of the god pots and is removed when the gods pots are old and die. After they are killed, the god pots are deposited in a cave. The cave I visited is the second of two caves that are used for this purpose. It is about an hour's walk east of the village and is about forty feet long and five feet high. I counted twenty-one god pots there, and believe them to be the incense burners replaced in the most recent incense burner renewal ceremony in 1993.

## God Houses

The final ritual place in traditional Lacandon religion is the god house. As I learned about ancient Mesoamerican astronomy and architecture I hoped to find that god houses were in some way mini-reflections of Lacandon cosmology. After all, the ancient people of Mesoamerica were well versed in the movements of the sun, planets, and stars, and constructed many buildings as observatories to mark various astronomical events. Edges of doorways and windows, horizontal and vertical shafts, sight lines between edifices of sculpted monuments, and even the arrangements of different buildings were architectural devices used by ancient

Mesoamerican peoples to make astronomical observations. For example, the Governor's Palace at Uxmal and Temple 22 at Copán were oriented for observing the appearance and disappearance of Venus (Aveni 1980:245). There also are structures, such as the Caracol at Chichén Itzá, that were built specifically to mark a variety of astronomical phenomena (Aveni et al., 1975; Aveni 1977).

Like the ancient Maya, Lacandon in Nahá used a cosmological orientation in the construction of their ritual buildings, albeit on a more modest level. It is vitally important for Lacandon god houses to face the east because the god pots must face Yaxchilan. Consequently, when constructing a god house, the practitioners of traditional religion would align the building's center ridge pole to point at Polaris, the North Star. This alignment provided the appropriate eastern-facing orientation for the entrance to the god house. Chan K'in Viejo's god house is shown in Figure 5.4.

I also discovered that the directional orientation of the homes in Chan K'in Viejo and Matejo Viejo's house compounds duplicated the orientation of the god house. The community of Nahá was originally located on the northern shore of Lake Pethá,

**FIGURE 5.4**    Chan K'in Viejo's god house, 1982.

moving to its current site in 1979. I was present soon after the construction of Chan K?in Viejo's god house and homes in the new location. When I measured the orientation of the god house, cooking huts, and the homes built within the elder men's house compounds I found that they all followed the same directional orientation, with virtually all of the original structures being aligned to the north. Lacking surveying instruments I could not measure the orientation of homes with mathematical precision. However, the Lacandon's own measuring device, sighting on Polaris, and a compass were adequate for determining a home's general directional orientation. Most of the structures' primary entrances were also on the east side, following the plan of the god house.

According to the observations of Maler and Tozzer, the head of every extended family they encountered maintained a god house in which he stored his god pots and made his offerings. By the time of my arrival in Nahá in 1980 there were only four god houses in use, with groups of related men sharing space and ritual implements; by 1999, there were just three. Correspondingly, most of the Lacandon homes today are aligned parallel to the road that was built through Nahá after the community relocated and do not parallel the orientation of the old god houses.

## Ritual Implements

Lacandon men communicated with the gods listed in Table 5.1 through incense burners called *läkil k?uh*, literally "god pots." The god pots were central to all Lacandon ritual activity because they were the medium of communication between gods and men, and the vehicle for transmitting offerings. During a ritual, gods were asked to descend to the god house and partake of their offerings when they are placed in the god pot dedicated to them. Typical offerings were items such as *pom*, or copal incense, tamales called *nahwah, chul ha?*, a corn drink, and balché. In return for these offerings, Lacandon men asked the gods to care for their families and crops. If family members were sick or a crop was doing poorly, it was typically blamed on a god's disappointment with a man for his lack of attention to the god. The god's displeasure could only be ameliorated by making the appropriate offerings.

God pots were conceived as corporeal replicas of the gods to whom they were dedicated and, like the *santos* of the Highland and Yucatec Maya, were thought to be alive. In fact, the culmination of the month-long incense burner renewal ceremony was the ensouling of the new god pots and the killing of the old. During their construction, five cacao beans were placed in the bowl of a new god pot to represent the heart, lungs, liver, stomach, and diaphragm. Specific facial features, such as ears with earrings, eyes, nose, and especially the mouth were molded on the head of the god pot. The front of a god pot is called its chest, and the bottom, its feet. God pots are painted white with vertical black stripes for males and crossing, vertical and horizontal stripes for females, representing the traditional woven smock. They are spotted red with annatto in the places that correspond to the forehead, chin, chest, and feet where men used to paint themselves during important ceremonies.

One of the most obvious features of a god pot is the prominent out-thrust lower lip on its face (see Figure 2.1, p. 37). This lip is deliberately oversized to serve as a receptacle for offerings of food and drink that were given to the gods during important ceremonies. Additionally, most men in the early 1980s burned offerings of *pom*, or copal resin incense, in the bowl of the god pot on a daily basis. The copal incense was used as food for the gods because it was thought to transform into tortillas when it was burned in the bowl of the god pot.

In addition to god pots, the *xikal*, or incense board was a vehicle for offering incense or rubber figures (see Figure 5.5). The incense board, which symbolically references human sacrifice, is a wide mahogany paddle that is stored in the god house rafters. Over the years, I watched Chan K'in Viejo teach several of his sons to make *xikal* offerings. Essentially, a man took small nodules of copal and one at a time placed them in rows lengthwise across the paddle. Each nodule of copal represented a part of the body, thus each row of incense was an abstract representation of a human being. When the rows of incense on the *xikal* were complete the petitioner stood holding the *xikal* before the god pots and recited a prayer to animate the people built on the *xikal*. The nodules of incense were then removed and burned in the god pots. These human offerings become messengers and helpers for the gods whose god pots received the offerings.

**FIGURE 5.5**   Chan K'in Viejo making a *xikal*.

## Types of Offerings

In addition to god pots and copal, practitioners of traditional Lacandon religion had a variety of ceremonial implements, inedible
offerings, and food to present to their gods. God pots and offerings were never placed directly on the ground. Instead, before a
ceremony, god pots were arranged on short hand-hewn mahogany boards called *pätähche'*. Offerings of food and gourds full
of *balché* (the gourds are called *hämäh*) were typically arranged on
beds of palm leaves in front of the god pots, with the gourds of
*balché* sitting on woven vine rings called *me'et*.

The largest ritual implement was the *balché chem*, the dugout
canoe in which *balché* is mixed and fermented. The *balché chem*
was hewn from a single log of mahogany and hollowed out with
an adze. It was prepared on the spot where the tree was felled,
then dragged to the god house clearing where it was placed parallel to the god house entrance resting on legs of crossed sticks. It
is just right of the god house in Figure 5.4.

*Balché* was served from a large clay vessel called a *pak* that
has the face of Bol, the Lacandon god of *balché*, modeled on one
side. The host of a ceremony ladled *balché* from the *chem* into the
*pak*, carried the *pak* to the god house, then filled individual drink-

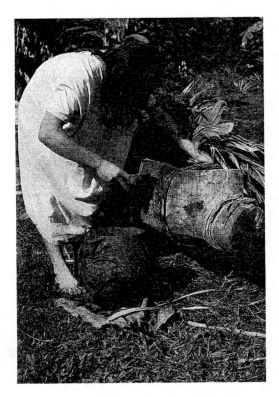

**FIGURE 5.6**   Filling the *pak* with *balché*
from the *balché chem,* 1983.

ing gourds from it (see Figure 5.6). The *pak* was also the vessel that
a man uses to fill the *balché chem* with water when preparing a
new batch of *balché*.

The most frequent offering to the gods was copal incense or
*pom*. Copal is pine resin incense that was extracted from local groves
of pine trees and pounded in a trough until it was the consistency
of oatmeal. Typically, copal was spooned from a bowl directly to the
incense burner, but it was also molded into conical lumps that were
placed in the incense burner. When burned, copal was said to be
transformed into *atole,* a sort of corn soup, or tortillas. In fact, a large
lump of copal looks remarkably like the big balls of corn dough
from which women make tortillas. In addition to copal incense, less
common offerings were small rubber figures called *k'ik'*.

*K'ik'* are also a form of symbolic human sacrifice. The *k'ik'* are
abstract rubber-like figures of men and women between one to two
inches tall. The name is derived from the Lacandon word for blood,

*kʔikʔel,* and they are fashioned out of rubber tree sap. The figures were made with human facial features and hair and typically burned with incense in a god pot after being displayed to the gods on incense boards. Before the figures were burned the ritual sponsor brought them to life with a chant that ensouled and awakened them. Davis gives the full text of one such chant she recorded in Nahá in 1974 (1978:137–141). After their consecration the *kʔikʔ* offerings were again displayed before the gods and then burned. As the figures burned they were said to ascend to the gods' layer of the cosmos and become domestic servants in the homes of the deities.

*Kuxuʔ,* a red vegetable dye made from seeds in the fruit of the annatto tree, is the source of the red pigment that was used to paint ceremonial garments, ritual implements, and even participants in important ceremonies. The Lacandon gods are pleased by the sight and smell of human blood, and turn of the century Lacandon pierced their earlobes with flint blades and dripped their blood in the god pots to appease their gods. However, by the mid-1900s, men started substituting the red dye for their blood.

*Kuxuʔ* is used in a variety of ways. Up until the 1970s, men painted their faces, wrists, and ankles with the dye. Decorative red spots were painted on the *balché chem* and certain areas in the god house. God pots were painted with alternating red and black stripes, and a young man wore an annatto spotted robe in the *mekchul,* a coming of age ceremony sponsored by his father.

Annatto was also used to dye strips of cloth called *chäk huʔun,* ("red paper"), which was made from the bark of the ficus tree. The bark cloth strips were typically about an inch wide and twelve to sixteen inches long. These bands were gifts to the gods and were cut or notched with diamond shapes that indicated the god to whom the *chäk huʔun* was dedicated. They were also worn by ritual participants and tied around the *balché chem* and the pot from which *balché* was served. When used this way annatto was a blood substitute for like the ancient Maya, Lacandon men formerly dripped their blood onto the bark cloth and burned it in their god pots.

## Edible Offerings

Most of the offerings discussed so far were prepared by men in the god house. Edible offerings were cooked by women in the ceremonial kitchen shelters that were constructed next to a god house. Most of these offerings were common foodstuffs that when prepared for ritual use took on sacred properties. Annatto, for example, is used as a seasoning. In a ritual context, however, it became human blood. Similarly, *ma'ats*, the ground corn drink that is typically eaten at breakfast or for a midday snack, in the god house became *chul ha'*, meaning "sacred water." *Chul ha'* was the most frequent food gift to the gods. Like *balché, chul ha'* was dripped first onto the mouth of the god pots, then gourdfuls were distributed to the men in the god house. Once the gods and men had been served, the rite's sponsor carried gourdfuls of the drink to his wife. She, in turn, passed out gourds of *chul ha'* to the women watching the ceremony from the cooking hut.

Säk ha', or "white water," is the ceremonial form of the corn drink *ma'ats*. Although a common offering, I never saw it offered alone. Instead offerings of *säk ha'* were typically accompanied by gourds of *balché*. The ritual sponsor's wife made *säk ha'* by grinding corn and mixing it with water in a sieve over a pot. The thick corn residue at the bottom of the pot was removed, squeezed into corn dough balls, and roasted. The remaining liquid was then boiled in a smaller pot, and cooked until it was thick. The *säk ha'* was then poured into gourd cups where it was distributed to the ceremony's participants and the women watching the rite from their cooking huts.

From time to time the gods demanded a payment of *nahwah*, small, square-shaped, ceremonial tamales that are cooked in banana leaves. Ideally, *nahwah* were filled with monkey meat but in recent years were more commonly filled with beans. Tamale offerings were made in sets of five. The fifth tamale in each set was marked with a strip of palm leaf, thought of as the "mouth" of the tamale. When they were presented to the gods, pinches from these tamales were placed on the lip of the god pots. Davis (1978:205) says this palm strip was also called "Hachäkyum's bite."

After cooking, the sets of *nahwah* were placed in wide gourd bowls in front of the god pots to show the gods their offering. Then the gods were fed their tamales. The rite's participants took a pinch of tamale and placed it in the mouth of the god pot. When the gods were fed, each participant received a bowl or two of *nahwah*. After eating a few, he then took the rest to his wife who watched from the cooking hut. In turn, she took them home for the family to eat.

The final form of edible offering was *käkoh,* a bitter drink made from cacao beans. The beans were displayed to the gods the night before the drink was made. Small gourd cups, each containing five beans, were arrayed in front of the god pots for the gods to see. The next morning the ritual sponsor's wife roasted the beans on a griddle and ground them by hand with a *mano* and metate. While grinding the beans she added a grass she called simply *aak,* which is Lacandon for "grass." The sap in the grass made the liquid foam once water was added and the mixture was agitated with a grooved mallet. After the mixture was strained through a gourd colander, it was ready to drink.

*Käkoh* was a secondary offering in that it was not drunk straight but was mixed with the rite's principal offering, such as *säk ha².* When the *käkoh* was ready the sponsor's wife brought cups of the liquid chocolate to the god house, sat down and frothed it by twirling her chocolate beater back and forth between her hands. When the drink was foamy, the sponsor took the cup from his wife and poured it into cups of *balché* or *säk ha²,* after which it was offered to the gods and then drunk by the male participants in the rite. Davis (1978:216) provides the text of a song for chocolate drink preparation.

## Ritual and Agriculture

I participated in my first Lacandon religious ritual on July 14, 1980, within a few days of arriving in Nahá. This was followed by a second on July 16 and the third on July 17. From the beginning of my time in Nahá I was immersed in their ritual practices. Given this introduction to Lacandon society it is not surprising that my interests focused on Lacandon religion. At the time, I did not understand the basic types of ritual activity or the role that agriculture played in religion.

To my knowledge, Davis (1978:252) was the first to outline the four basic types of Lacandon ceremonial activity. First are the god pot renewal rites, a yearly activity at the turn of the century, held only every five to ten years by 1980. The last god pot renewal rite was conducted in 1993 before Chan K²in Viejo's death. Second are the *Ya²ahk²in, Na²ahplil, Witsbir, Chulha²ki²,* and *Tikin*

*Wah* ceremonies, which are formal payments to the gods for curing a sick person. Third are first fruit offering ceremonies called *ts? aik u ho?ol,* and, fourth, what Lacandon men call *pokik u bäh,* to "burn incense for oneself." This last ceremony is the simplest, the most common, and was practiced by individual men on a daily basis. In this ceremony, usually conducted in the morning or late afternoon, a man simply burned incense in selected incense burners and asked the gods to grant members of his family good health. He passed a couple of *bo?oy* (palm leaves twisted together) through the smoke of the incense and tucked the leaves in the wall near a person's bed so that the gods could see the subject of the prayer and the patient could see he or she was being prayed for.

Although I was thrust into the ritual life of the men in Chan K?in Viejo's compound from my first days in Nahá, it was only much later that I understood the fundamental role that agriculture played in Lacandon cosmology and religion. In the 1980s, I perceived *balché* to be the central element in Lacandon religion. It was not until I began studying agriculture in the 1990s that I came to understand that while *balché* was a significant offering, much of the underlying purpose of ritual and the cosmological significance of the rites was based on the Lacandon agricultural cycle. On an individual basis men burned copal incense daily to feed the gods and maintain their deities' goodwill. Virtually all the large communal rites, on the other hand, were devoted to the well-being of the *milpa.*

The *u ho?ol u bäkel,* or "the head of our bodies," ceremony was conducted at the beginning of the corn planting season in April and May. The name refers to feeding the substance of our bodies (corn) to the faces on the god pots. The rite was conducted to ensure a good corn crop, and was primarily a ceremony in which *chul ha?* was fed to the god pots.

More common than the corn planting ceremony were the *u tsaik u ho?ol,* or "give to the head" rituals. These were first fruit ceremonies that were prepared from the first harvest of the main crops planted in a *milpa.* Because the traditional Lacandon farmer planted so many crops, these ceremonies were held year-round. In the case of corn, which is the most important crop, the first fruit offerings were even held for several of the foods that are made from corn. Thus over the course of the agricultural year, one might typically have seen Lacandon households sponsoring a series of rituals such as

| | |
|---|---|
| *u ho?ol kuuts* | tobacco offering |
| *u ho?ol ik* | chili offering |
| *u ho?ol buul* | bean offering |
| *u ho?ol nahwah* | tamale offering |
| *u ho?ol chäkbil nal* | boiled new corn offering |
| *u ho?ol wah* | corn tortilla offering |
| *u ho?ol kayem* | corn drink offering |
| *u ho?ol päkbil näl* | roast corn offering |
| *u ho?ol säk ha?* | corn drink offering |
| *u ho?ol kum* | squash offering |

The *u tsaik u ho?ol* ceremonies were simple compared to some of the curing rituals. In general, they involved the head of the household feeding the god pots the specified food offering and praying for the god to accept it. *Balché* offerings were not typically a part of these ceremonies. I participated in several of these rituals in the early 1980s. They were typically conducted by men in Chan K?in Viejo's or Matejo Viejo's families. However, thanks to the observation made by Dale Davis in 1974, I know that that these first fruit offering rites were in decline by the time I first lived in Nahá. Davis recorded these rites as almost monthly events (Davis 1978). In my time in Nahá I recorded less than a dozen and know of only two families and one individual who have held these ceremonies in the last few years. However, before the 1980s, these simple rites formed the core of Lacandon ritual practice.

The significance of agriculture in Lacandon cosmology was brought home to me in a classic fieldwork situation that has probably been experienced by all field anthropologists, that is, the dramatic flash of intuitive insight to which the natives shrug their shoulders and say "of course." The relationship between agriculture and ritual was so obvious to the Lacandon men I worked with that no one ever mentioned it. My eyes were opened to the role of agriculture in Lacandon cosmology on the night of January 31, 1995. After dinner, Chan K?in Viejo and I were discussing the story of Chäk Ik Al's destruction of the earth. In this story, Hachäkyum decided his creations were defective and should be destroyed. He asked the Red Wind Lord of the East, Chäk Ik Al, to destroy the world. Chäk Ik Al obliged Hachäkyum's request, first sending a powerful wind that ripped trees out by their roots and shredded the Lacandon's homes. Then when everything lay in ruins on the ground, Hachäkyum started a terrible conflagration that consumed all of the debris. Following the fire Chäk Ik Al brought a torrential rain that covered the earth in water in six days. The only people, plants, and animals to survive this great destruction were those few who were sheltered in a dugout canoe by the lord of the *milpa*, Äk'inchob. After two years, the water receded and when the sun came back out Äk'inchob replanted the forest and the remaining humans planted their *milpas* and repopulated the earth (for more on this myth see McGee 1989 and 1997).

Sitting there with Chan K'in Viejo it suddenly struck me that the myth was describing the Lacandons' cycle of slash and burn horticulture. In essence, the myth was modeled on the natural cycle of corn farming. In the myth, the Lacandon undergo the process which they impose on the environment every spring. Chäk Ik Al fells the forest, Hachäkyum burns it, and his son-in-law Äk'inchob replants the forest and human beings with the "seed stock" he saved in his canoe. When I mentioned this parallel to old Chan K'in Viejo he replied, "Of course," and reminded me that humans were made from clay and corn and that it is Äk'inchob, whose name translates as "corn kernel priest," the lord of the *milpa* who saved human beings. It was then I understood that agriculture was fundamental to Lacandon religion and that making *milpa* was a reenactment of creation. When I finally understood the relationship between Lacandon religion and agriculture the decline in rituals started to make sense. In the last few decades as tourism became increasingly important at the expense of agriculture, the rituals associated with the agriculture lost much of their value and fell into disuse.

## Healing and Ritual

In addition to agricultural rites, the other main class of Lacandon rituals was payment rituals held to reward the gods for curing a seriously ill person or aiding in the birth of a child. Chan K'in Viejo told me that men need to pay the gods periodically with offerings of copal, food, and *balché*. If a man ignored these offerings, the neglected gods would get angry and cause members of his family to fall ill. In such a situation, the therapeutic action was to diagnose which god was angry through a divination ceremony and make that god the appropriate offerings. If the offerings appeased the god's anger, he or she would cure the afflicted individual.

As with the agricultural rites there are a variety of these ceremonies called the *Ya²ahk²in, Na²ahplil, Witsbir, Chulha²ki²*, and *Tikin Wah*. The *Ya²ahk²in* ritual was the most elaborate of these rites, second only to the month-long god pot renewal ceremony. The *Ya²ahk²in* was a payment to the gods for curing someone who was seriously ill and featured a wide variety of ritual offerings including *balché, chul ha², kuxu², nahwah*, cacao, copal incense, and *k²ik²*. The full rite could take several days to complete and typically encompassed shorter ceremonies carried out on consecutive days. The first day's ceremony, for example, might have featured offerings of copal and corn drink. The second day the participants burned incense and drank *balché*. On the third day the rite's sponsor might have offered *xikals*, burned rubber figures, or fed the god pots tamales.

The *Na²ahplil* ceremony was also held to pay the gods for healing someone who was ill or assisting in the birth of a child. I could not differentiate between the *Na²ahplil* and *Ya²ahk²in* ceremonies except perhaps that the quantity of offerings was not as large in the *Na²ahplil* rite. The purpose of the two ceremonies and the offerings made to the god pots were the same.

The *Witsbir* and *Chulha²ki²* ceremonies were to pay the gods for cures. They were the least complicated of the ceremonies. Typically, the only offerings were *balché* and copal incense. The two were also the most social of the ceremonies as they involved larger groups of men and the consumption of large quantities of *balché*. Most of the rites that I participated in and called *balché* rituals in my 1990 book were one of these two types.

The last therapeutic ritual was the *Tikin Wah* or *Tikin Nahwah* ceremony. This ceremony was a payment to the gods to ensure the continued good health of a family member. Typical payments were ceremonial tamales, copal incense, and *balché*.

One nonritualized form of healing that has survived the decline of Lacandon religious observance is the use of medicinal plants. Gertrude Duby Blom (1969:296) and Dale Davis (1978:37) both claimed that the Lacandon did not use or have any knowledge of medicinal plants. I always found this a curious statement given the Lacandon have such a detailed knowledge of the forest, but accepted it at face value until I started inventorying plants in 1996 and found that the Lacandon identify numerous medicinal plants that grow wild in the forest as well as those plants they learned about from neighboring Tzeltal Maya. The healing plants used by some Lacandon families and the ailments they treat are described in the next chapter.

## The End of the World

In the spring of 1995 and summer of 1996, Chan K'in Viejo recited the complete cycle of creation and destruction stories for me, and his sons helped me with my transcription and translation of the stories. Unlike the Christian conception of a benevolent God, the Lacandon's creator is capricious and has destroyed his creations three times. In the earliest episode, Hachäkyum summoned everyone to his home at Yaxchilan. There Hachäkyum collected the people together and according to the story, he hung them from the rafters, slit their throats, and collected the blood in a huge clay pot. He then conducted a divination ceremony with the blood and used it to paint the god's homes. The corpses were thrown to the giant jaguars and snakes he keeps as pets.

According to Chan K'in Viejo, we know of these events today because one individual, named Hawo', escaped. Hawo' was swallowed by one of Hachäkyum's serpents but cut his way out of its belly with a flint blade he had hidden in his hand. He then climbed the Milky Way through the layers of sky to Hachäkyum's sky where he begged the gods to spare his family. Mercy was granted when Hawo' promised to make the gods offerings of *balché* and *nahwah*. Thus Hawo' lived to tell the tale and his family repopulated the earth.

The story of Chäk Ik Al combines the second and third destructions of human beings. As described earlier in this chapter, the world was first consumed in a great fire and then drowned in a great flood of rain.

The final destruction which is yet to happen will occur when Hachäkyum orders his son T'uup to hide the sun under his *xikul* in a permanent eclipse. Everything will then perish in the cold and dark. Hachäkyum's giant jaguar pets, the *Nah Tsulu*, will eat us, and our souls will sit in darkness with the *Chembel K'uh*, or minor gods. Interestingly, the ancient Maya also believed solar and lunar eclipses were evil omens. They thought that disasters were likely to occur during eclipse episodes, thus great trouble was taken to chronicle and predict their occurrences. Among my Lacandon friends the knowledge that solar and lunar eclipses were imminent caused some anxiety. Dan Renshaw was in Nahá for the major solar eclipse on July 11, 1991. He told me that people had heard about the upcoming event on the radio and were very concerned. When the moon began to obscure the sun people restrained their dogs, went into their homes, and closed and latched all doors and windows. People did not reappear until the light had returned to normal. Chan K'in Viejo told me that during an eclipse, Hachäkyum gives T'uup permission to cover the sun with his smock so that Hachäkyum can see whether his creations are behaving properly. Eclipses are warnings. If Hachäkyum is displeased by what he sees he may give permission to end the world. However, by 1995, the solar eclipse visible in the Lacandon area on April 25 passed virtually unnoticed by people in Chan K'in Viejo's house compound because many people had seen television programs explaining the earth and moon's orbit and eclipses in astronomical terms. Young people with a television induced Western view of their world were not concerned with eclipses. Some individuals were interested in the novelty of glimpsing the eclipse through welder's glass that I had bought for that purpose, but the event itself caused little notice.

Chan K'in Viejo believed that the final destruction would occur when the forest was completely destroyed and predicted that it would be soon. I am not mystically minded, and the Lacandon I know are not waiting in fear for the world to end; however, there is some metaphorical truth in Chan K'in Viejo's words. If the forest is destroyed, the agricultural way of life on which their culture has been based will also disappear. As it is, recent economic events have played out in tandem with the shunning of traditional agricultural rituals.

## The Demise of Religion

I suspect that the shift to a commercial economy was instrumental in the demise of traditional religion. In particular, this economic change is associated with several elements that may have contributed to the decline in religious practices. First, much of Lacandon religion was associated with agriculture, such as ceremonies to ensure good harvests and bring rain for crops. In the last decade, as commerce with tourists has started to compete with agriculture, the cycle of agricultural ceremonies lost purpose and the rituals were abandoned.

Second, the other great class of Lacandon rituals was associated with curing. As Lacandon households began to generate significant incomes, they were able to seek effective medical care at private clinics in Palenque and San Cristobal. In particular, pregnant women began to seek prenatal care and give birth to their babies in San Cristobal. As Lacandon families began to take advantage of Western medical facilities, there was a corresponding decline in the practice of rites for healing and therapeutic incantations. In many societies it has been difficult to provide Western medical intervention because nonindustrial people's ideas of sickness and healing are often related to their religious beliefs. The Lacandon, however, did not hesitate to adopt a Western medical view of sickness and treatment at the expense of the rituals that formed the core of their traditional therapeutic strategies. This topic will be dealt with in more detail in the next chapter.

Third, a primary school was built in Nahá in the summer of 1996 that many boys and girls now attend. Several parents told me they thought knowing how to read, write, and do math were important skills that their children needed for the future. The children receive basic literacy and math training in addition to Mexican history, social studies, and other subjects. Thus the mythic worldview that explained the cosmos and the place of humans in it is being replaced by a secular, Western view of the world.

Finally, I believe television, brought to the community in 1993, also contributed to the demise of Lacandon religion. This occurred at two levels. First, children now play games based on the cartoon characters they watch on television rather than memorizing the traditional knowledge of the elders. In any nonliterate society if the youngest generation does not learn the accumulated wisdom of their elders, then that knowledge is irrevocably lost within one generation. Further, television opened a view of a much larger world than most Lacandon possessed prior to its introduction. Lacandon people knew there was a larger world outside of their jungle. I, for example, came from "across the ocean." But television brought that world into their homes. And this world did not obey the rule of the Lacandon gods. Mythology was inadequate to explain huge cities, modern warfare, global economic trends, and other aspects of the modern industrial world. The Lacandon for the first time had to face the relative insignificance of their society and traditional beliefs. As a result, within four years after the introduction of television traditional religious practice had virtually ceased to exist!

The Lacandon never formed a centralized political structure. Even living in larger communities they have continued to maintain an egalitarian society based on the autonomous household. In the absence of centralized political authority, shared beliefs and the communal practice of religious rites provided some measure of social cohesion. That common thread is now gone, leaving little more than the maintenance of traditional appearance in the pursuit of tourist dollars as a unifying force. Lacandon religion as I was taught it in the early 1980s has disintegrated. I cannot say what people believe in their hearts, for many individuals still remember the rites and prayers. I can only say from direct experience that these rites are regularly practiced today by the members of only two households and one other individual.

# 6

# The Decline of Traditional Healing Practices

As discussed in Chapter 5, the two great classes of Lacandon rites were directed at agriculture and healing. Chapter 5 focused on the decline in agriculture rites. In this chapter, I will discuss healing rituals, therapeutic incantations, and the use of medicinal plants. Through the early 1980s, Lacandon men in Nahá spent a great deal of time conducting rites that were directed toward asking a god to cure sick family members or were payments for a past cure. Today, these rites have been abandoned just as conclusively as the agricultural rites discussed in the previous chapter. However, I want to begin this chapter by describing the healing rituals I witnessed and the use of therapeutic incantations. After this initial discussion I also outline a discovery I made with my student Belisa Gonzaléz in 1996, and investigated with the help of my students Ryan Kashanipour, Jessica Roe, and Kathy Tipton in 1998 and 2000. In direct contradiction to previously published reports (Duby-Blom 1969; Davis 1978), we discovered that some Lacandon families in the communities of Lacanha and Nahá make extensive use of forest plants for medicinal purposes. So while the religious rituals associated with healing have been abandoned, many Lacandon continue to use plants to treat traditional illnesses in addition to accepting Western forms of medical intervention.

## Lacandon Categories of Sickness

Although descriptions of illness vary from person to person, in general Lacandon men and women I spoke with divided illness into a limited set of categories with names primarily derived from

**TABLE 6.1    Lacandon Disease Terms**

| Term | Symptoms |
|------|----------|
| *tsem* | Upper respiratory infection |
| *säk tsem* | Respiratory infection with mucous discharge |
| *chäk wilil* | Fever |
| *kʔakʔil* | Skin inflammations, rashes, and measles |
| *yah in hol, bakel* | Headaches or body/bone aches |
| *chibal hämnen* | Stomachache |
| *hubil hämnen* | Diarrhea |
| *xeh* | Vomiting |

a person's symptoms (see Table 6.1). The most common illness was *tsem*. Symptoms of *tsem* correspond to what most Americans would call a cold, flu, or upper respiratory infection, including nasal congestion, cough, fever, and related body aches. Related to this is *säk tsem*, or "white *tsem*," which refers to an upper respiratory infection where the sufferer also has a cough and heavy mucous discharge. All fevers are called *chäk wilil*, or "seeing red," which refers to the red flush one sees in the face of a person with a high fever. *Kʔakʔil*, or "being on fire" (a bad translation but the best I can do), refers to inflammations of the skin, rashes, and measles. *Yah in hol* literally means "pain in my head" or to have a headache. *Chibal hämnen* is a stomachache and literally means a "bite in the intestines." *Hubil hämnen* means "disturbed" or "upset intestines," and refers to diarrhea. Finally, *xeh* means "vomiting."

## Curing through Prayer

Western medicine became readily available to the Lacandon of Nahá in the late 1970s when several rural clinics were built in the Lacandon Jungle. However, most community members still discussed disease and treatment in religious terms into the 1980s. In the popular view of that time, illness was usually sent by an angry god to punish a person who had ignored the god by neglecting to make the appropriate offerings. In this type of illness the appropriate treatment was to conduct a divination to discover which god was angry, then appease the irate deity with offerings of incense.

Another approach was to appeal to a different deity to intervene with the angry god on your behalf and request that the disease be taken back. At the same time, the appropriate therapeutic incantations were recited to ease the afflicted person's symptoms. Except for those diseases thought to be brought by outsiders and for which Western medicine was appropriate, all diseases were considered to be supernatural in origin and were treated by ritual activities conducted in the god house. Although I initially did not understand much of what was going on in the god house shared by Chan K'in Viejo and Matejo Viejo, looking at my notes from those first visits it is now clear that much of the daily ritual activity I watched was directed toward curing or preventing illness.

Many Lacandon also recognized that some illnesses were spread by contact with outsiders. Most typically Tzeltal from neighboring communities were blamed for spreading sickness. However, foreigners who visited their villages were also sources of contagion. Measles, flu, and other illnesses brought by contact with outsiders were caused by Äkyantho', who is the god of foreigners. Äkyantho' also made medicine to treat these illnesses and these remedies were acquired from nearby Tzeltal communities, Palenque, or San Cristobal. According to Chan K'in Viejo, the Lacandon gods were not much help with these afflictions because the diseases were not familiar to them.

The Lacandon have enthusiastically acquired medicinal concoctions since at least the early 1900s, typically, patent medicines brought from nearby *monterías*. Davis described men administering penicillin injections and aspirin in the early 1970s (1978:53). In 1980, I saw Lacandon men openly administer medicines they had acquired in Palenque or from the local clinic, and I was constantly asked to read the directions for various vitamins and over-the-counter medicines that people had bought, or which had been left with them by well-meaning visitors. However, despite this unofficial doctoring, men still attempted to cure family members by asking gods to intercede.

One of the most common activities I witnessed in my early years in Nahá was men burning copal and holding palm leaf wands, called *bo?oy*, in the thick smoke of the burning incense. Having previously identified the god who was angry, the man would chant an apology and promise that if his family member were cured he would sponsor a ritual and pay the god *balché*, copal, and ritual foodstuffs. In Chan K?in Viejo's household, the aid of Hachäkyum and Äk?inchob was often enlisted to speak to some vengeful deity on behalf of the supplicant who was burning the incense. After the prayer session the smoked palm leaves were usually tucked into the wall of the house near the bed of the sick person so that the gods could better find and heal him or her.

## Therapeutic Incantations

Some Lacandon men also know therapeutic incantations in which the words themselves have the power to heal. If a person knows the appropriate incantation he does not necessarily have to ask the gods for help. The beneficial effects of the words could be felt within a few minutes simply by reciting the incantation and then blowing on the patient. Curing incantations were used for headaches, stomachaches, nausea, childbirth, even bleeding. Davis (1978:45) discusses watching Chan K?in Viejo recite an incantation over a boy who had almost amputated a toe in a machete accident and claims the bleeding quickly stopped. I also saw Chan K?in perform one of these chants to assist his wife in the birth of their son Chan K?in (#24) in June 1981. Although I was not allowed to witness the birth, I watched Chan K?in run back and forth from his house to the god house most of that afternoon. I assumed something was wrong. Late in the day, I saw him emerge from his house with a serious look on his face, and walk alone into the forest with something wrapped in leaves in his arms. I thought the child had died during the birth and he was disposing of the body. A couple of days later Chan K?in invited me into his house to see "my son." "It must be yours," he joked, "because the baby has white hair and light eyes." In fact, the child has white-blonde hair and pale skin, and it remains a joke to this day that Chan K?in, (#24) or *säk hool* ("white head"), is my son. The package Chan K?in carried into the forest that day was the placenta which he disposed of in secret so that no one could use it to magically harm the new baby.

Few men admit to knowing or using healing incantations. These chants are considered dangerous because if they are not recited properly the person attempting the incantation may be harmed. I was lucky that Chan K'in Viejo knew several healing incantations and did not mind if I listened when he used them. He was not, however, interested in teaching me any incantations because he felt that with my imperfect Maya I might harm myself. Consequently, I never recorded any incantations. The only incantations for which I have found transcriptions include one recorded by Davis for caterpillar stings (1978:47–52) and one by Boremanse (1979) who recorded an incantation to prevent vomiting. I hope to record more incantations in future work in Nahá as I gather more information about Lacandon conceptions of disease and medicinal plants.

## Curing Strings

The use of therapeutic incantations and making payments to the gods for cures are both activities that are highly ritualized and conducted solely by men in the god house. There are two other forms of curing, however, that are conducted by women and which have no associated ritual activity. These are the use of curing strings and medicinal plants. Married women make curing strings for family members and friends, or even a favorite dog, who falls ill or is injured. The women spin cotton by hand into a string, which is tied around the sick person's neck or the injured limb. One reason only married women prepare curing strings is that they are associated with the umbilical cord, which is considered powerful and carefully disposed of after birth. The Maya love plays on words and the curing strings are called *k'uch* which rhymes with the Maya word for umbilical cord, *t'uch*.

As I understand it, the string has therapeutic value because it is something like a charm, and women give the strings to prevent harm from returning to them. Dan Renshaw, a friend who is married to a woman from Nahá, once told me that if a woman hears of someone who is sick and does not give the person a string, and her negligence contributes to that individual's death, then the soul of the dead person may return and seek revenge.

Stay in Nahá for a good period of time and you will see virtually everyone at one time or another wearing curing strings, which he or she leaves on until the string disintegrates. In particular, I usually see multiple strings on children and babies. My own experience with the curing strings came in the summer of 1996 when my wife, Stacie, pregnant with our first child, traveled with me to Nahá.

The journey to Nahá can be arduous under the best conditions and riding in the dust and exhaust of a pickup truck in the summer heat are not the most comfortable travel arrangements for anyone, least of all someone who is pregnant. By the time we arrived in Nahá, Stacie was exhausted and sick to her stomach. After the introductions and initial exchange of pleasantries she retired to our quarters to lie down. However, the pleasure expressed by the women in Chan K'in Viejo's house compound when they met Stacie soon turned to concern when they learned that she was nauseated, had taken to her hammock, and was not interested in eating. Kohs III and IV asked how Stacie was feeling several times that evening and were concerned that she did not want to eat. I think they were truly alarmed the next day when she still didn't feel like getting up and eating anything and had trouble keeping down the broth and tea they made for her. That day the Kohs and one of their older daughters (#11) made curing strings and brought them to Stacie to wear and I secretly started planning ways to get her back to Palenque for medical care. We all were relieved when Stacie's stomach settled down and her appetite returned. By the next day women were sitting down to tell us stories of their pregnancies and deliveries.

## Medicinal Plants

One morning in 1996, when inventorying plants in an elderly woman's *milpa*, I discovered by accident that some Lacandon use medicinal plants. One of my students, Belisa Gonzaléz, was interested in studying the lives of Lacandon Maya women and we were visiting elderly widows who supported themselves. As one woman showed us her *milpa* and identified the plants she was cultivating she casually pointed to one, *tsak wohen* ("lemon grass"), which she said one could boil in water and drink for a stomachache. I was astounded. I had never before heard of anyone using medicinal plants. I asked if she had any more plants in her *milpa* that had medicinal properties and she showed me *ino²*, possibly anise, that could also be boiled in water and drunk as a tea to soothe an upset stomach. She also pointed out a plant she called *tsak bak²*, or "bone medicine." She said that one could boil the leaves in water and then rub the liquid on one's aching legs.

We didn't pursue information on medicinal plants in 1996, but I came back with three students in the summer of 1999 to look specifically at medicinal plant use in Nahá and among an enclave of Northern Lacandon living in Lacanha. In all we discovered over two dozen plants that different Lacandon identified as having medicinal value. However, we also discovered that some plant identifications were idiosyncratic, that is to say that one person used the plant but others did not. Consequently, in our identifications we accepted only those plants that were also identified as medicinal in other works that discuss Lacandon agriculture and plant use. In particular, Nations and Nigh's 1980 survey of Lacandon agricultural techniques and Ignacio March's 1998 summary of plants and animals used by the Lacandon were valuable sources of information. Less helpful was an undated but recent report by Maria Fadiman on medicinal plants used in Lacanha. In this report Fadiman identifies several plants as being used for cancer, diabetes, and arthritis, which are not Lacandon disease categories and were probably supplied by ethnobotanists who worked in Lacanha in the mid-1990s. Additionally, not understanding Maya, Fadiman identified the Lacandon names of several plants as names that translate as "another vine," "another tree," "red vine" and "red tree." Still we were able to correlate a couple of the plants we found with those listed in her report. Table 6.2 summarizes those plants whose identifications are found in our work and at least one of these reports. Because the information was gathered in different Lacandon communities at different times we are confident they represent an accurate list from which to start the study of the Lacandon's knowledge of medicinal plants.

I list the plants in Table 6.2 by the symptoms they treat because many of the plants overlap Lacandon disease categories. A

**TABLE 6.2** Lacandon Medicinal Plants

| Symptom | Lancandon | English/ Spanish | Scientific Name |
|---------|-----------|-----------------|-----------------|
| Fever | *Mäx Ak* | ? | ? |
| | *Pahok* | *Guatipil* palm | *Chamaedorea sp.* |
| | *Chi Keh* | ? | *Chrosophyllum mexicanum* |
| | *Puuna* | Mahogany | *Swietenia macrophylla* |
| Diarrhea/ Upset Stomach | *Chäkah* | Palo mulatto | *Bursera simaruba* |
| | *Moak té* | Ficus/amate | *Ficus sp.* |
| | *Pesa* | Wild clove | *Eugenia caryophyllata* |
| | *Chak Che* | ? | ? |
| Nausea | *Känse ak* | ? | ? |
| | *Ko'och* | Mulberry | *Cecropia peltata* |
| Worms | *Kächex* | Goose foot ? | ? |
| Bone and Muscle Aches | *Nikte Ak* | Wild clove | *Eugenia caryophyllata* |
| | *Chäkax* | Palo mulatto | *Bursera simaruba* |
| | *Chi Keh* | ? | *Chrsophyllum mexicanum* |
| Cough | *Mulix* | Lime | *Citrus aurantifolia* |
| | *Äh thus* | Wild grape | *Vitis sp.* |
| Che chem | *Päsak* | Ginger | *Costus sp.* |
| Wounds | *Bäbah* | ? | *Sapindus saponaria* |

Items marked with question marks are those that I am not conclusively able to identify.

bad case of *tsem*, for example, would probably include a fever, body aches, and a cough; therefore, several of the Lacandon helping us tended to list plants in more than one category. Most of the treatments involve chewing the leaves or bark, or boiling a plant's leaves or bark, and drinking the resulting liquid. To treat worms, for example, we were told to eat a handful of leaves from the plant *kächex* (the name means "you have worms"). For a cough we were told to boil the roots of a wild grape (*äh thus*) and drink the liquid three times a day. However, some treatments are more direct. To treat nausea one chews the bark of the vine called *kanse ak*. Contact with the *che chem* tree (*Sebastiania longicuspis*) can produce almost unbearable blistering and itching that is treated by squeezing the juice from a stalk of *päsak*, a type of ginger, onto the afflicted area. For a fever, our guides told us to chew a piece of stalk from the *pahok* plant, or several leaves from a plant called *chi keh*. A plant called *bäbah* noted by both Nations and Nigh (1980) and Fadiman is prescribed to help heal wounds. The treatment is to collect and dry leaves from this small tree, grind them into a powder, and sprinkle the powder on the wound.

I have been describing how I gathered information in Nahá and Lacanha, but Ryan Kashanipour, Kathy Tipton, and Jessica Roe returned to Lacanha to pursue this topic in greater detail and were able to find a wider variety of plants in Lacanha than I initially encountered. Because I was not in Lacanha with them but have used some of the information they gathered I asked Ryan to write a brief description of his fieldwork experience.

> In the summer of 1999, I made my first trip into the Lacandon Jungle with Dr. McGee and two other students, Kathy Tipton and Jessica Roe. One of the goals of our trip was to investigate Dr. McGee's 1996 discovery of medicinal plants, which he made in the Northern Lacandon community of Nahá. We conducted our research among an extended family group of Northern Lacandon who live in the Southern Lacandon community of Lacanha Chan Sayab. Our research took place in two phases. In the first phase, we sought to confirm McGee's initial discovery and prove that Lacandon families used medicinal plants. In the second phase, we attempted to record the Lacandon names and uses of medicinal plants and the ailments they treated.
>
> While in Lacanha, we conducted our research within the family compound of Jorge Chan K?in. Five of Jorge's children, all of whom have husbands or wives and families of their own, lived in the compound, which totaled about thirty people. We were able to work with Jorge and four of his sons and sons-in-law.

We worked only with men, quite simply because they seemed to have free time. On the other hand, many of the Lacandon women were busy with continuous household chores and were therefore less accessible. For the most part, the men had already planted their *milpas* and answering questions posed by three Americans struggling with the Lacandon language seemed to provide a considerable amount of entertainment.

Our research was conducted through informal interviews. We asked a series of health and medicine questions that centered on how each individual treated illness. In general, the men were responsive to these questions and revealed that they used plants from the jungle to cure sickness. However, when asked about the specifics of medicinal plants, many individuals hesitated sharing information. Often we were sent in circles between individuals. On one occasion, Jorge claimed that his son-in-law Vincente grew and used numerous medicinal plants and that we should talk to him if we wanted information. When we approached Vincente, he responded that he knew little about the medicinal plants, but that his brother-in-law Enrique Chan K?in used them extensively. Enrique, in turn, maintained that he did not use any plants for medicine and said that his father, Jorge, was the person who knew the most about medicinal plants.

In the end, Jorge proved to be both our most valuable informant and the most reluctant individual to share information. Initially, Jorge seemed skeptical about our interest in his use of plants. He claimed that he knew of only a few plants that were useful. However, Jorge revealed over a dozen medicinal plants on a jungle hike; several of which he cultivated in his *milpas* and in abandoned gardens. His collection of medicinal plants ranged from *äh thus* (wild grapevines) and *mulix* (lime trees) to *puna* (mahogany fruit). Moreover, his preparation and usage varied from simply eating the leaves of *kächex* for worms to slowly boiling the fruit and leaves of *ton k'uk* for three days and drinking the liquid to treat a fever.

Overall, our investigation revealed that some Lacandon in Lacanha readily cultivate and use medicinal plants. We did not encounter any curing specialists in Lacanha, unlike the numerous h-men or shaman found in the Maya communities of the Yucatán. Instead, each household seemed to use the plants in their own way. Additionally, healing with medicinal plants did not appear to be ritualized in any manner. The Lacandon we interviewed used medicinal plants as a means to treat illness when other methods were not available and there did not appear to be any supernatural implications in the use of these plants. In general, knowledge of how to survive in the jungle permeates Lacandon society and healing with plants from the jungle seems to be a natural part of this knowledge.

As with therapeutic incantations, I feel that I have only scratched the surface of the information on medicinal plants that is possessed by Lacandon men and women. The difference between the two is that the use of medicinal plants is an active tradition practiced by men and women, whereas the knowledge of therapeutic incantations is limited now to just a few older men who are reluctant to discuss them. Both subjects deserve further investigation.

Information on the intellectual property rights of the knowledge of indigenous peoples, in particular healers, has recently become a controversial topic in anthropology. For example, a recent edition of *Cultural Survival Quarterly* was devoted to this topic (Vol. 24(4), 2001). In Chiapas the question of who has the rights to this information and stands to profit from indigenous knowledge of medicinal plants has been publicized because of the objection of Maya groups to the "bioprospecting" of anthropologists and pharmaceutical companies.

I wish to emphasize that we were not bioprospecting for plants that may have medicinal properties. We are aware of the conflicts that have been generated in Chiapas by some scholars' pursuit of the knowledge of indigenous Maya healers. The focus of our project was to understand Lacandon conceptions of disease and the ritualized treatment of these ailments using plants and incantations. We were not interested in whether the plants used in healing rituals actually contained therapeutic compounds that would be of interest to Western pharmaceutical companies. Even if I had the training to conduct the kind of chemical and medical research that has gone on in other parts of Chiapas, I believe that Lacandon traditions are their property to be used in a manner that the Lacandon deem appropriate. If a profit is to be made from their knowledge of medicinal plants, it should be the Lacandon who collect the checks.

## The Decline of Healing Rituals

As with other ritualized aspects of Lacandon culture the treatment of disease through religious rituals has virtually disappeared. I know of only two men who continue to practice the ritual cures and therapeutic incantations they learned from their fathers, although isolated families who continue these traditions may certainly exist. The decline of agricultural rituals discussed in Chapter 5 is easy to link with the move that most Lacandon have made to a more commercial economy at the expense of traditional agricultural practices.

But what about the healing rituals? Why have most families also abandoned these? Maybe the first and most practical response to this question is that as Lacandon households began to earn extra income with the sale of tourist goods they were able to seek effective medical care in the private clinics in Palenque and San Cristobal. In particular, pregnant women began to seek prenatal care and give birth to their babies in San Cristobal. Considering the discussion of infant mortality and maternal mortality associated with childbirth in Chapter 3, it should be no surprise to anyone that young men and women sought the chance to take extra steps to ensure their health and their babies' safety as medical care became available.

The establishment of a chain of rural clinics in the late 1970s accelerated this process. Many women who would not travel to Palenque or San Cristobal for medical care now found that basic services could be provided in their community. As young Lacandon families began to take advantage of Western medical facilities, there was a corresponding decline in their practice of rites for healing and therapeutic incantations. Older men like Chan K'in

Viejo continued to practice the traditional religious therapies for their children but increasingly this was done in tandem with visits to the clinics or medical specialists in San Cristobal.

In many societies it has been difficult to provide Western medical intervention because nonindustrial people's ideas of sickness and healing are often related to their religious beliefs. However, although traditional Lacandon beliefs about illness were linked with their religious beliefs, they showed no hesitation in adopting Western medical therapies that were used side by side with the religious forms of treatment. Older men like Chan K⁷in Viejo could accept the use of Western medical therapies because many maladies fell under the authority of Äkyantho⁷. In this manner they incorporated the new ideas into their religious beliefs. But as young Lacandon men began to abandon the ritual activities that were traditionally their responsibility, they also turned their backs on religious definitions of disease. Today, virtually all families in Nahá use home remedies or visit the community clinic for minor problems and travel to see doctors in San Cristobal when dealing with serious threats to their health. In fact, the Asociación Cultural Na Bolom in San Cristobal has established a medical fund to help defray the costs of medical care for Lacandon who seek medical treatment there.

Thus just as new economic opportunities contributed to a shift in agricultural practices and the accompanying religious rituals, so too the economic boom in the 1970s that brought clinics to the jungle and tourists to Chiapas contributed to the decline in traditional religious therapies. As Western medical care became more accessible and young Lacandon families had the money to purchase that care, they paid less attention to the traditional healing rituals with the result that today, thirty years later, virtually no one practices the therapeutic incantations or offering rituals by which men used to protect the health of their families.

# CHAPTER

# 7 Twenty Years among the Lacandon: Some Lessons Learned

Twenty years of learning about the Lacandon, thinking about the events in their lives, and writing about the things I have seen has taught me larger lessons about life and the discipline of anthropology. First and foremost, I believe that the heart of the anthropological enterprise is fieldwork. Research in the library and classroom has its place, but books and slides cannot substitute for direct experience. In particular, my Lacandon experiences have shown me the limitations of the discipline as I was taught it in school. Concepts such as objectivity and cultural relativity that are so clear in a classroom get quite messy in the field. The most intricate theoretical models, so precise on paper, will break down in the day-to-day reality of life as you experience it in a fieldwork setting. And the setting is constantly changing. An approach that yields clear explanations of behavior one year, may become gibberish the next. In my own work I have found that the patterns which seem so clear in one time and place can be fundamentally different in a different year. To sort things out one needs to be in the field year after year, generation to generation.

## What Is Lacandon Culture?

So what does this say about the most fundamental of all ideas in anthropology, the concept of culture? The history of cultural anthropology is a history of ethnographic studies based on different notions of culture. I began my work with the Lacandon studying traditional Lacandon religion as it was practiced by a group of about twenty men in the community of Nahá. At that time, my idea of culture was that it was a belief system carried in the minds of the Lacandon and acted out in rituals. However, I finally came to the realization that the Lacandon culture I studied only incorporated the activities of men. What about the other half of the population?

Lacandon women led my work in a different direction and ultimately to a different concept of culture. While men were praying in front of god pots in their god houses, women were weeding *milpas*, grinding corn, washing clothes, and caring for children. These activities, less esoteric than the ritual activity I had been watching, ultimately proved more interesting and led me to a much deeper understanding of Lacandon life. Working in a *milpa* with Chan K'in Viejo and his wives taught me that the basis of Lacandon religion was the agricultural cycle. Pulling weeds, shelling corn, and cooking tortillas taught me as much about Lacandon spirituality as watching men burn incense in a god house.

Further, looking at the material aspects of Lacandon life over the last five years has ultimately led to a much more profound appreciation for Lacandon lives than the previous fifteen years I spent studying religion. For one thing, the religion in which I invested so much time has disappeared. My book *Life, Ritual, and Religion among the Lacandon Maya* is now a historical curiosity concerning ritual practices in the 1980s, but has little current relevance to life in the Lacandon Jungle. My present focus on the material aspects of Lacandon life is an ongoing enterprise that incorporates agriculture, tourism, money, men and women's work, medicinal plants, and scores of other topics. Best of all, these aspects of Lacandon life are all interrelated parts of a living system that is continually changing and adapting to life within a much wider context than religion. Oil, tourism, NAFTA, the Mexican government's policy toward the Zapatistas, the price of beef, and the attempts of environmental organizations to preserve the rain forest all factor into life in the Lacandon Jungle. It is a life's work to try to grasp what is happening in Lacandon society.

So what is Lacandon culture? I don't think there is a set answer. Lacandon culture is what the Lacandon think, feel, and do, and what the Lacandon think, feel, and do encompasses a wide variety of beliefs and activities that change all the time. To be sure you can find beliefs and activities common to most Lacandon, but for every common aspect of culture you can also find a difference. Virtually all Lacandon speak Maya, but they do not consider Maya a definitive element of their identity. Virtually all Lacandon watch television when they have an opportunity to do so, eat tortillas, and have sold things to tourists at some point in their lives. But these cultural traits are hardly diagnostic of Lacandon culture. Some Lacandon have long hair, some have short hair. Some Lacandon wear traditional style clothing, some wear jeans and T-shirts. Some are kind, some are not. Some are faithful to their spouses, some have affairs. Some are honest to a fault, others are unscrupulous. Some treasure their children, others have abandoned them. Some Lacandon are shy and chaste, others have fathered or borne children out of wedlock. At least one Lacandon has taken the life of another in Nahá. All these aspects are part of the living reality of Lacandon life, or life in any community.

I have worked with the Lacandon Maya for twenty years and I still cannot define Lacandon culture with any precision. This dilemma has lead me to question the utility of the idea. Culture seems to be whatever we want it to be, depending on the theoretical background on which we base our work. If I cannot define Lacandon culture for a group of six hundred people, how is it possible to talk of culture in a nation such as the United States that has millions of people and tremendous ethnic diversity? Many anthropologists claim that anthropology is a science but few sciences have their core concepts so poorly defined.

My experiences in the Lacandon Jungle have also led to a profound distrust of much of the writing that is carried out in the name of anthropology. Many of the ethnographies I see are based on fieldwork conducted one or two decades ago. They are snapshots of a society in time, but that time is passed. How accurate are they today? I have seen recently published works written about the Lacandon that were based on work conducted in the 1970s. Many aspects of the Lacandon society they describe no longer exist. If different theoretical approaches yield different results and the ethnographic setting changes from year to year, then maybe Franz Boas was right. Anthropology is inherently historical and ethnographies are history in disguise.

# What People Say Is Different from What They Do

Another interesting aspect of the anthropological enterprise is that what people say is often different from what they do. This is a classroom axiom in anthropology, but what are the implications for understanding a society? Whole branches of anthropology are based on what informants have said they believe or do. But what if informants in all sincerity tell you something, they believe what they said, but later you see that their actions contradict their words? Which version of their culture is true? For example, in a discussion with the Kohs about Lacandon gender roles, Koh III emphatically stated that making *milpa* was men's work and that women did not do it. Five minutes later she told me a story about how much she enjoyed going to work in the *milpa* with Chan Kʔin Viejo when they were young. Also, I had watched her work in the family *milpas* for over fifteen years.

So, is reality what people say it is, or what they do? I think the answer is a resounding "Yes to both! " However, in my work now I rarely take a person's word at face value. I watch to see if the individual's actions support what he or she says. If the words and actions don't match, then a whole new avenue of exploration opens up. Wouldn't it be interesting to know why Koh III denies that women do the work in which she engages on a daily basis?

# Marriage, Fatherhood, and My Position in the Community

In addition to watching what people do as well as listening to what they say, I have learned that what you are allowed to see and hear has a great deal to do with how you are defined by the people with whom you work. Male or female, single or married, parent or childless, all are intimately related to the questions you think to ask, the answers you get, and the people who will speak with you.

I have come to realize that the significance of events you experience in a fieldwork setting has as much to do with who you are and what is going on in your life as that setting. As I look back

I realize that Chan K'in Viejo accommodated me in his household and supported my early work in religion in large part because I was a young unmarried man. Essentially he took me in as an adopted son. Although twenty-four, I lived with his teenage sons because socially I was an adolescent. Religion was an appropriate topic for me to study because I was male, and he taught me side by side with his own sons. Once I learned which were food plants and which were weeds, I was a welcome source of *milpa* labor for his household as most of Koh IV's children were too small to do much work. Also, as I described in Chapter 3, because I was a young unmarried man, virtually all interaction with the women in the compound was carried out through their husbands, fathers, or brothers. If I had been a woman I imagine my experiences would have been dramatically different.

When I married, in 1994 at the age of thirty-eight, my position in the community changed and there was a subtle shift in how people treated me. As an adult I was given my own house to rent rather than staying in the young men's quarters. In god house rituals I was offered a seat with the other adults instead of sitting with the adolescents at the periphery. I also found that the women in Chan K'in Viejo's compound were much more willing to interact with me.

In addition to the events in your life affecting your field experience, the needs of your informants also come into play in the roles you take in a field setting. I spent most of the spring of 1995 in Nahá and found myself increasingly asked to participate in household activities that are typically the responsibility of the head of a household as Chan K'in Viejo physically declined in what was the last year of his life. When Chan K'in Viejo was too sick to join his family at dinner the Kohs offered me his place at the table. I was increasingly asked for medical advice, to read prescriptions, and to show his wives the proper dosages to administer. As a married man I could joke with Chan K'in Viejo and his wives and was included in the circle of gossip whenever something happened in the community. I became closer to Chan K'in Viejo at the end of his life, in large part, because he saw me as someone who cared about the traditions to which he had devoted his life. In his final years it must have been clear to Chan K'in Viejo that he represented the end of an era. The majority of men in Nahá, including most of his own sons, had not continued to practice the traditional rituals after he was too frail to do so and he saw in me a way to save and pass on some of his knowledge. In the spring of 1995, he spent hours every day with me reciting myths and stories that I would transcribe on the spot. He often spoke of how I would tape these stories so that his grandchildren could hear them. In this case, Chan K?in Viejo's needs were just as instrumental in the material I was able to gather as my own interests.

Bringing my wife, Stacie, to Nahá in 1996 and becoming a father not only caused a major change in the types of questions in which I was interested, but also redefined with whom I could talk about those questions. Stacie's presence removed many of the barriers between me and the women in the compound. With Stacie and my student Belisa González, I was able to document women's activities in detail. We discussed pregnancy and childbirth, menstruation, and sex, and I suddenly found myself invited into people's homes to watch *telenovelas* at night. I had a discussion with a teenage girl about kissing (Lacandon think it's gross), and having boy- and girlfriends, and she confided that a friend was pregnant by a Mexican soldier stationed nearby. Further, raising my own children has given me a new appreciation for following the births and deaths of babies in the community and the resources people have to support their children.

## Involved Objectivity or Why I Ran into a Burning House to Look for Someone Else's Children

When I began my fieldwork in Nahá, I believed that I was there to observe, to be objective, and record events as I saw them. I didn't feel that people's problems were my concern. I wanted things to go well for the people I worked with but I didn't feel much of a responsibility to help when things went badly. Getting involved would limit my objectivity and I felt I shouldn't interfere. One of the best examples of this attitude occurred in 1981 when I discovered that Koh IV's son Chan Kayum was seriously ill. I found out that Chan Kayum was ill when I saw Chan K?in Viejo diligently working on a set of offerings in the god house. When I asked what he was doing Chan K'in said his son was sick, and when I saw Chan Kayum he was obviously suffering. I asked Chan K'in Viejo if he was going to take Chan Kayum to the doctor in Palenque or San Cristobal and he said no. I thought a trip to the doctor might be in order but shrugged and thought, "Well, it is not my kid so it isn't my responsibility." Fortunately, the boy recovered.

Crises have helped me shed the detachment with which I approached the Lacandon in the first years of my fieldwork. A defining moment took place in early February 1995 when the Mexican army moved large numbers of troops into the Lacandon Jungle to try to contain Zaptista forces that were hiding in the forest. With no warning, we were confronted with the sight of columns of troop transports, tanks, armored personnel carriers, and trucks towing artillery rolling through the community to a newly established base near Monte Libano. We all shared a concern that the troops would stop in Nahá and that there might be fighting near the community. Things became very real to me when I was helping one of Chan K'in Viejo's sons-in-law prepare an offering in the god house and a helicopter gunship circled the structure to take a closer look. I stepped outside the shade of the god house to let the pilot have a clear look at me and stood there waving while looking into the weapons in the nose of the helicopter hovering above us. Then the helicopter climbed away and left us alone again. That day white flags sprouted up all over the community to proclaim our neutrality in the conflict, and after years of detached observation I felt that for once I was a part of what was happening in Nahá rather than just studying events.

Today I no longer try hard to be objective or believe that the problems of Nahá are not my own. Part of this change has to do with Chan K'in Viejo's decline and death, another part has to do with becoming a husband and father. Chan K'in Viejo's health failed at a time when my career was advancing and I found that I had the resources to help him and his family. Since his death in 1996 I consider it part of my responsibility to help his family when I can. Today the people of Nahá are no longer just sources of data, they are my friends. I think the best way to illustrate the change in my attitude and what it means for me is to tell one last story. What you are reading is taken from my notes about the events of the night of June 9, 1999, written down the following morning.

6/9/99

About 10:15, as I was getting ready for bed, I heard a tearing/crashing sound and then yelling coming from down the hill. My first thought was that a truck's parking brake had released and someone's truck had rolled through the wall of a house. Then I heard a woman screaming. I grabbed my shoes and ran outside, looked down the hill and saw a terrible, unmistakable orange glow over the trees at the base of the hill. My old translator and roommate K'in's house and store was on fire. I took my flashlight and yelled to the Kohs in the next house that I was heading down the hill to help.

When I got down to the house I could see a crowd of men, shadows against a background of flame, carrying propane gas cylinders out of the house and struggling to move two big oil barrels full of gasoline away from the fire. I helped shove one drum of gasoline away from the house, then ran to the front of the house to help with the propane tanks. I found a man wrestling with a cylinder that was still hooked to a stove. We had no wrenches to uncouple them, so I lifted the stove and we carried them out together to the edge of the yard. I remember thinking how hot the fire was and I wondered if we had moved the gas far enough away. People were yelling, the fire roaring, and everything was lit in an unearthly shade of orange. I noticed someone else fighting to roll another drum of gasoline away from the fire but he was stuck on something. I ran over and together we heaved it up and rolled it away from the house.

Then I saw Victor, a guide for volunteers from Na Bolom, in the yard calling into the house. We ran into the half of the house not yet on fire and called in. Was anyone inside? Did anyone need help? We didn't see anyone, so we ran back out into the yard and found someone holding K'in's wife Maria. She was screaming that her baby was inside. Victor and I turned to escort her away, telling her that no one was inside, when she broke free and ran straight back into the house. I ran after her, caught her before she got too far into the fire, and had to force her back out of the house. I told her that I had seen her children down by the school but she was frantic and insisted her baby was inside. So I went back in. I didn't really think about it. I just had a vision of a child hiding in a burning room so I went back in to look. I crawled into a bedroom, looked at the flames on the roof, and started repeating to myself shit, shit, shit over and over. I couldn't find anyone. I went into the kitchen, no one there. I looked in the living room and behind a stack of chairs. No one. It was hot, the stench of burning plastic was everywhere, no kids. I ran back out and Victor and I carried Maria away from the fire. Down at the school we found her husband and children who were frantic because they didn't know where she was. They had a tearful reunion which turned to sobbing that everything they had was lost. K?in's older brothers Kayum and Bol kept repeating to them that everyone would help them and that they would be ok.

I walked back up to the house but there was nothing left to do. It was engulfed in flames. Then bullets that K?in sold in the store starting exploding, I remembered the propane tanks, and I ran back down the hill away from the house. Everything was bright orange light and dark shadows and explosions from the house drove everyone farther back.

At this point, about 11:30, I thought to go back to my house and let the women know that everyone was safe. I got up to the compound and found it completely dark and empty. All the women and children in the compound had fled. I started looking for them. Walking down a dark trail in a nearby *milpa* I heard crying and muffled voices. I found them hiding in a shelter in a *milpa*. The glow of the fire and the bullets exploding had convinced them that the Zapatistas were attacking and they had grabbed the kids and run to hide. Further, they were convinced that I had been killed when I ran down the hill and were as surprised to see me as I was to hear they thought the village was under attack.

Although I assured them that everything was all right they were afraid to return home because every few minutes a can of food from the store would explode and they were convinced the explosions were from weapons. It took about an hour to talk the group into going home. It was about one in the morning before everyone returned home and we were kept up most of the night by the cans of food detonating in the fire.

I was up at 6:30 to survey the damage (see Figure 7.1). There was not much left but a concrete slab and twisted sheets of tin from the roof. K'in's friends started emptying out his store's warehouse shed and converting it to a temporary house. At 3:00 as the afternoon rains rolled in, K'in had a new, albeit, smaller house, and we were waiting on the return of a group from Ocosingo who went to get clothes, shoes, and other necessities to get the new household started.

**FIGURE 7.1**    K'in's house, June 10, 1999.

I find that today I am no longer much interested in the Lacandon as sources of data. I am still interested in their lives and the changes occurring in their society, but I am no longer dispassionate about events in Nahá. I have learned that I can be objective and honestly report on events in Nahá without being detached from the people. I care very much about what happens to the people there and feel a responsibility to help when I can.

The Lacandon have given me much more than I have returned. I have grown up with one foot in their society and another in the United States and have built a career based on information they shared with me. Although my work with them has led me to question some of the basic aspects of my chosen field, the Lacandon of Nahá have helped me become a better anthropologist and a better man. As I start the second half of my career, I find that I am much more interested in how my work can be to their benefit, rather than how it benefits me. This book is a start in that direction.

# Three Generations of
# Chan Kʔin Viejo's Family

Keeping track of children's births and deaths was difficult in Nahá. The deaths of newborns are never mentioned, and when recounting family history parents would not mention the deaths of older children. It was only when I systematically went through all twenty years of my field notes that I realized there were babies whose births I recorded in the 1980s who were not alive in the 1990s. This chart is the most complete record I could make of Chan Kʔin Viejo's wives, children, and grandchildren. It is based on family histories and my own notes. I have listed them by their Maya names and the number designation (e.g., Chan Kʔin Tercero) their family gave them.

## Key to Generations I and II

1. Chan K?in Viejo (d. 12/23/96)
2. Koh I (d. 1930s?)
3. Koh II (d. 12/25/84)
4. Koh III
5. Koh IV
6. Chan Nuk
7. Nuk
8. Chan K?in
9. K?in
10. Chan K?in Tercero
11. Nuk
12. Chan Nuk (died with infant)
13. Chan Nuk
14. Kayum
15. Chan Nuk
16. Bol
17. Chan K?in Quatro
18. K?in
19. Chan Nuk
20. Chan K?in Quinto (d. 1999)
21. Nuk (d. 8/5/93)
22. Kayum
23. Bol
24. Chan K?in Sexto (b. 6/9/81)
25. K?in (b. 10/84)
26. Chan Nuk (b. 1985)
27. Chax Nuk (b. 1987)
28. Chan K?in (b. 1993)

**Generations I and II**

# Generations II and II

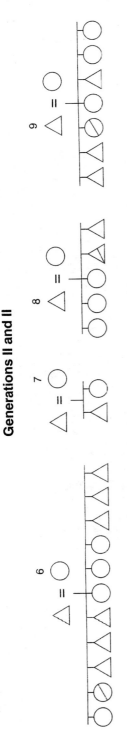

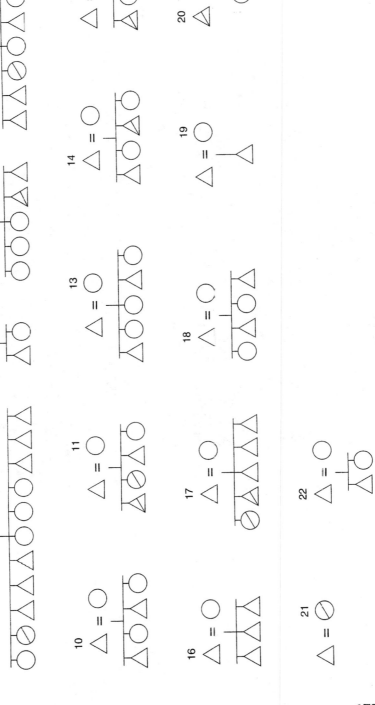

# GLOSSARY

**Äk'inchob**   Lacandon lord of the *milpa.*

**Äkyantho'**   Lacandon god of foreigners.

**atole**   the Spanish name for a corn drink (see *säk ha'*).

**Audiencia**   the court of law through which the Supreme Council of the Indies governed. It consisted of a president, four judges, and a prosecutor.

**ba'ay**   a net bag woven from the fibers of the agave plant.

**bo'oy**   a wand made of guatapil palm that is used in curing ceremonies.

**bäk nikte**   the plumeria flower. In Lacandon mythology the Lacandon gods were born in the plumeria.

**balché**   a ceremonial mead made by fermenting a mix of water, honey, and the bark of the *balché* tree (*Lonchocarpus longistylus*).

**bo'oy**   a palm leaf wand used in curing ceremonies.

**caribal**   turn-of-the-century term for a Lacandon house group. The term is derived from the word *caribe*, which the Lacandon used to refer to themselves when speaking Spanish.

**chäk hu'un**   bark cloth headbands made from the bark of the ficus tree. Typically dyed red with annatto.

**Chäk Ik Al**   Red Wind Lord; god of the east who brings hurricane winds and rain.

**chulha'**   a ritual form of *ma'ats,* a corn drink (see *ma'ats*).

**Chul ha'ki'**   name of a Lacandon curing ceremony.

**chem**   a dugout canoe, or the container in which *balché* is brewed.

**entrada**   an armed expedition into Indian territory.

**finca**   plantation.

**Hachäkyum**   Lacandon creator deity.

**Hach Bilaan Hachäkyum**   the statue of Bird Jaguar IV in Structure 33 at Yaxchilan.

**Hach Winik**   "Real" or "True" people. What the Lacandon call themselves.

**hach T'an**   "Real" or "True" language, or Lacandon Maya.

**hämäh**   the gourd cup in which *balché* is served.

**Hawo²**    character in a Lacandon myth who survived a destruction of the world, and traveled to the realm of the gods in the sky.

**hetzmek**    The Lacandon rite of passage featuring ritualized instruction of adult roles.

**ho²ol u bäkel**    a Lacandon ceremony at the beginning of the corn plant-ing season in which *ma²ats* is fed to the god pots and the gods are asked to provide a good corn crop.

**incensario**    Spanish term for an incense burner.

**kah**    the Lacandon term for other Indians.

**kanche**    the Lacandon word for bench or seat: also the stone placed in the bowl of a god pot during its construction.

**käkoh**    a ceremonial drink made by mixing ground cacao beans, water, and the sap of a grass.

**k²ik²**    humanoid figures made of natural rubber that are burned as of-ferings in god pots.

**Kisin**    Lacandon god of the underworld who causes death and pun-ishes the souls of those who misbehave.

**k²uch**    cotton string; also the curing strings made by Lacandon women.

**kuxu²**    a red dye made from the seed pods of the annatto or *achiote* plant. The dye was used as an offering and to paint ritual imple-ments, headbands, and garments.

**ladina/ladino**    a girl or boy who is of Indian heritage but is Mexican in cultural background.

**läkil k²uh**    a Lacandon god pot, or incense burner.

**league**    in the eighteenth century, a league was roughly three miles, or the distance one could walk in an hour.

**ma²ats**    corn gruel made from rough ground corn mixed with water. Soft boiled corn is ground into dough and mixed with water over a gourd sieve. Sugar, honey, or cacao may be added to flavor the drink, which can be served hot or cold. The residue from the sieve is fed to chickens.

**Maseca**    an instant tortilla mix widely marketed in Mexico.

**me²et**    woven vine rings on which are set gourds of *balché*.

**mekchul**    a coming of age ceremony in which a father thanks the gods for his son's or daughter's survival to adulthood.

**Menche Tunamit**    Sapper (1897) describes the Lacandon as making religious pilgrimages to this site; today it is called *Yaxchilan* (see Yax-chilan).

**Mensäbäk**    Lacandon god of rain.

**molino**  a metal hand grinder used to grind corn kernels.

**montería**  a logging camp in the forest.

**milpa**  the Spanish name for a swidden garden; *kol* in Lacandon

**Na'ahplil**  name of a Lacandon curing ceremony.

**Nah tsulu**  giant celestial jaguars who are the pets of *Hachäkyum* (see Hachäkyum).

**nahwah**  a ceremonial meat- or bean-filled tamale.

**oh'**  reeds used for making the shafts of arrows.

**onen**  a clan animal name that is inherited from one's father.

**pak**  the clay vessel out of which *balché* is served into individual drinking gourds.

**pak che kol**  an abandoned *milpa* left fallow.

**päkbil wah**  a baked tortilla crisped over a fire.

**pätähche'**  the boards upon which god pots are arranged before a ceremony; the word literally means "wood on which something is left."

**pixan**  soul or spirit, also can refer to the pulse or heartbeat.

**pokik u bäh**  the daily offering of incense and prayers in which a man asks for the gods to grant his family health.

**pom**  copal incense.

**reduccion**  the resettlement of Indian populations into mission communities.

**säk bel äk yum**  the Milky Way; literally the "white road of our lords." The Milky Way is the path the gods take to travel between different layers of the cosmos.

**säk ha'**  literally "white water," or in Spanish *atole*; this corn drink is prepared like *ma'ats* except that the liquid is cooked longer and stirred until it reaches a thicker consistency.

**säkpet**  a large ball of corn dough.

**Säkäpuk**  one of Hachäkyum's assistants.

**Sukunkyum**  Lacandon lord of the underworld and judge of souls. Hachäkyum's older brother.

**telenovelas**  Mexican soap operas.

**Tikin Wah**  a Lacandon curing ceremony.

**to'ohil**  Lacandon Maya religious leader.

**ts'aik u ho'ol**  Lacandon first fruit offering ceremony.

**tsul**  Lacandon term for a European or American man (see also *xuna'an* and *kah*).

**t'uch**  Lacandon word for umbilical cord.

**Tʔuup**   Hachäkyum's son; his job is to carry the sun through the sky.

**uuh**   Lacandon seed necklaces.

**Witsbir**   a Lacandon curing ceremony.

**xate**   leaves of the *guatapil* palm (*Chamaedoria spp.*).

**xikal**   an incense board.

**xikul**   traditional long, one-piece, Lacandon garment.

**xunaʔan**   Lacandon term for a European or American woman.

**Yaʔahkin**   a Lacandon curing ceremony.

**yalam luʔum**   the underworld.

**yatoch kʔuh**   "god house," the thatch-roofed structure where Lacandon men stored their incense burners and other ritual paraphernalia and conducted religious rites.

**Yaxchilan**   A Classic Period Maya city built at a bend of the Usumacinta River. Many Lacandon believe the structures at Yaxchilan are the homes of their gods.

# REFERENCES

Amram, David W. (1942). "The Lacandon, Last of the Maya." *El Mexico Antiguo*, Tomo VI(1–3):15–30, México.

Arizpe, Lourdes, Fernanda Paz, and Margarita Velázquez. (1996). *Culture and Global Change: Social Perceptions of Deforestation in the Lacandona Rain Forest in Mexico*. Ann Arbor: University of Michigan Press.

Aveni, Anthony F. (1977)." Concepts of Positional Astronomy Employed in Ancient Mesoamerican Architecture." In *Native American Astronomy*, edited by Anthony Aveni, 3–19. Austin: University of Texas Press.

———. (1980). *Skywatchers of Ancient Mexico*. Austin: University of Texas Press.

Aveni, Anthony F., Sharon L. Gibbs, and Horst Hartung. (1975). "The Caracol Tower at Chichen Itza: An Ancient Astronomical Observatory." *Science*, 188, 977–985.

Berendt, C. H. (1867). "Report of Explorations in Central America." *Smithsonian Institution Report for 1867*, 420–426.

Blom, Franz. (1944). "Statistics on the Lacandones." *Boletín Indigenista*, Vol. IV(1): 60.

Boddam-Whetham, John. (1877). *Across Central America*. London: Hurst and Blackett.

Boremanse, Didier. (1979). "Magic and Poetry among the Maya: Northern Lacandon Therapeutic Incantation." *Journal of Latin American Lore*, 5(1): 45–53.

———. (1998). *Hach Winik: The Lacandon Maya of Southern Chiapas Mexico*. Institute for Mesoamerican Studies Monograph #11. Albany, NY: University of Albany.

Boyle, Fredrick. (1867). "On the Free Indian Tribes of Central America." *Transactions of the Ethnological Society of London*, 6: 207–215.

Bruce, Robert D. (1974). *El Libro de Chan Kin*. Mexico, D. F.: Instituto Nacional de Antropología e Historia.

Bruce, Robert D., and Victor Perera. (1982). *The Last Lords of Palenque*. Boston: Little, Brown.

Bruce, Robert D., and Enrique Franco Torrijos. (1991). *Maya Art: Splendor and Symbolism*. Mexico, D. F.: Fondo Editorial de la Plastica Mexicana.

Cancian, Frank. (1987). "Proletarianization of Zinacantan, 1960 to 1983." In *Household Economies and Their Transformation,* edited by Morgan D. Machlaclan, 131–142. Lanham, MD: University Press of America.

———. (1992). *The Decline of Community in Zinacantan.* Stanford, CA: Stanford University Press.

Charnay, Desiré. (1887). *Ancient Cities in the New World.* London.

Chiapas! (1997). "Anuncia Ruiz Ferro inversion de más de 122 mdp para la selve lacandona." *Miércoles,* 28 de Maya: 11.

Clendinnen, Inga. (1982). "Yucatec Maya Women and the Spanish Conquest: Role and Ritual in Historical Reconstruction." *Journal of Social History,* 15(3): 427–442.

Cline, Howard. (1944). "Lore and Deities of the Lacandon Indians, Chiapas, Mexico." *Journal of American Folklore,* 57: 107–115.

Collier, George A. (1975). *Fields of the Tzotzil: The Ecological Basis of Tradition in Highland Chiapas.* Austin: University of Texas Press.

———. (1989). "Changing Inequality in Zinacantan: The Generations of 1918 and 1942." In *Ethnographic Encounters in Southern Mesoamerica,* edited by Victoria R. Bricker and Gary H. Gossen, 111–124. Austin: University of Texas Press.

———. (1994). *Basta: Land and the Zapatista Rebellion in Chiapas.* Oakland, CA: Institute for Food and Development Policy.

Davis, Virginia Dale. (1978). *Ritual of the Northern Lacandon Maya.* Unpublished Ph.D. dissertation, Tulane University, New Orleans, LA.

De Vos, Jan. (1980). *La Paz de Dios y del Rey: La Conquista de la Selva Lacandona: 1525–1821.* Mexico: Fonapas Chiapas.

———. (1992). "Una Selva Herida de Muerte. Historia Reciente de la Selva Lacandona." In *Reserva de la Biosfera Montes Azules, Selva Lacandona: Investigacion Para su Conservacion,* edited by Miguel Angel Vásquez Sánchez y Mario A. Ramos Olmos, 266–286. Mexico: Publicaciones Especiales Ecosfera No. 1.

Duby, Gertrude, and Franz Blom. (1969). "The Lacandon." *The Handbook of Middle American Indians,* Vol. 7, 276–297. Austin: University of Texas Press.

Ehlers, Tracy Bachrach. (1990). *Silent Looms: Women and Production in a Guatemalan Town.* San Francisco: Westview Press.

Fadiman, Maria. (n.d.). *Plantas Medicinales de Lacanja-Chansayab.*

Flood, Merielle K. (1994). "Changing Gender Relations in Zinacantán, Mexico." *Research in Economic Anthropology,* 15: 145–173.

García Moll, Roberto, and Daniel Juárez Cossío. (1986). *Yaxchilán: Antología de su Descubrimiento y Estudios.* Mexico City: Instituto Nacional de Antropología e Historia, Serie Arqueología.

Hellmuth, Nicolas M. (1970). *A Bibliography of the 16th–20th Century Maya of the Southern Lowlands: Chol, Chol Lacandon, Yucatec Lacandon, Quejache, Itza, and Mopan.* Occasional Publications in Anthropology-Archaeology Series #2. Museum of Anthropology, University of Northern Colorado.

———. (1972). "Progreso y Notas Sobre la Investigación Etnohistórica de las Tierras Bajas Maya de los Siglos XVI a XIX." *América Indígena,* 32(1): 179–240.

"Intellectual Property Rights: Culture as a Commodity." *Cultural Survival Quarterly,* 24(4): (Winter 2001).

Leutenegger, Benedict, and Marion A. Habig (eds.). (1976). *Nothingness Itself: Selected Writings of Ven. Fr. Antonio Margil.* Chicago: Franciscan Herald Press.

Maler, Teobert. (1903). *Researches in the Central Portion of the Usumasintla Valley.* Memoirs of the Peabody Museum of American Archaeology and Ethnology, Harvard University. Vol. II, No. 2, 22–40.

March, Ignacio J. (1998). *Los Mayas Lacandones, Hach Winik: Problemas y potenciales para el desarrollo de un grupo indígena minoritario.* Proyecto Perfiles Indígenas de Chiapas. ECOSUR—El Colegio de la Frontera Sur.

Maudsley, Alfred P. (1889–1902). *Biologia Centrali-Americana, Archaeology.* London.

McGee, R. Jon. (1989). "The Flood Myth from a Lacandon Maya Perspective." *Latin American Indian Literature Journal,* 5(1): 68–80.

———. (1990). *Life, Ritual, and Religion among the Lacandon Maya.* Belmont, CA: Wadsworth.

———. (1997a). "The Narrative Structure of Lacandon Maya Creation Myths." *Latin American Indian Literature Journal.* 13(1): 1–20.

———. (1997). "Natural Modeling in Lacandon Maya Mythology." In *Explorations in Anthropology and Theology,* edited by Frank Salamone and Walter Adams, 175–190. New York: University Press of America.

———. (1998). "The Lacandon Incense Burner Renewal Ceremony: Termination and Dedication Ritual among the Contemporary Maya." In *Sowing and Dawning in the Archeological and Ethnographic Record of Mesoamerica,* edited by Shirley B. Mock and Debra S. Walker, 41–46. Albuquerque: University of New Mexico Press.

McGee, R. Jon, and Kent Reilly. (1997). "Ancient Maya Astronomy and Cosmology in Lancandon Maya Life." *Journal of Latin American Lore,* 20(1): 125–142.

McGee, R. Jon, and Belisa Gonzaléz. (1999). "Economics Women and Work in the Lacandon Jungle." *Frontiers: A Journal of Women Studies,* 20(2): 175–189.

Nations, James D. (1979). *Population Ecology of the Lacandon Maya*. Ph.D. dissertation, Southern Methodist University, Dallas, Texas.

———. (1984). "The Lacandones, Gertrude Blom, and the Selva Lacandona." In *Gertrude Blom Bearing Witness*, edited by Alex Harris and Margaret Sartor, 26–41. Chapel Hill: University of North Carolina Press.

Nations, James D., and Ronald B. Nigh. (1980). "The Evolutionary Potential of Lacandon Maya Sustained-Yield Tropical Forest Agriculture." *Journal of Anthropological Research*, 36(1): 1–30.

Nations, James D., and Daniel I. Komer. (1982). "Indians, Immigrants and Beef Exports: Deforestation in Central America." *Cultural Survival Quarterly*, 6(2): 8–12.

Nations, James D., and John E. Clark. (1983). "The Bows and Arrows of the Lacandon Maya." *Archaeology* (Jan/Feb): 36–43.

O'Brien, Karen L. (1998). *Sacrificing the Forest: Environmental and Social Struggles in Chiapas*. Boulder, CO: Westview Press.

Palka, Joel W. (1998). "Lacandon Maya Culture Change and Survival in the Lowland Frontier of the Expanding Guatemalan and Mexican Republics." *Studies in Culture Contact: Interaction, Culture Change and Archaeology*, edited by James G. Cusick. Center for Archaeological Investigations, Occasional paper No. 25. Southern Illinois University.

Palka, Joel, and Nora López Olivares. (1992). "Sitios Lacandones Yucatecos en la Region del Rio Pasion, Peten, Guatemala." *U Tz'ib*, 1(3): 1–7.

Rich, Bruce. (1982). "Time Running Out for Mexico's Last Tropical Forest." *Cultural Survival Quarterly*, 6(2): 13–14.

Sapper, Karl. (1897). *Northern Central America with a Trip to the Highland of Anahuac: Travels and Studies of the Years 1888–1895*. Brunswick: Friedrich Viewig and Son.

Scholes, F. V., and R. L. Roys. (1968). *The Maya Chontal Indians of Acalan-Tixchel*. Carnegie Institution of Washington, Publication 560. Norman: University of Oklahoma Press.

Soto-Mayor, Juan de Villagutierre. (1983). *History of the Conquest of the Province of the Itza*. Frank E. Comparato (ed.). Culver City: Labyrinthos.

Soustelle, Jacques. (1933). "Notes Sur Les Lacandon Du Lac Pelhá Et Du Rio Jetjá Chiapas." *Journal De La Société Des Américanistes*, Nouvelle Série-Tome XXV: 153–180.

———. (1935). "Las Idees Religieauses des Lacandons." *La Terre et la Vie*, 4: 170–178, Paris.

———. (1937). *La Culture Les indiens Lacandons*. Tesis Doctorado, Univ. de Paris.

———. (1959). "Observations sur la Religion des Lacandons du Mexique Meridional." *Journal de la Societé des Americanistes*, XLVIII.

Stephens, John L. (1993). *Incidents of Travel in Central America, Chiapas, and Yucatan.* Washington, D.C.: Smithsonian Institution Press.

Tate, Carolyn. (1989)." The Use of Astronomy in Political Statements at Yaxchilan, Mexico." In *World Archaeoastronomy: Selected papers from the 2nd Oxford International Conference on Archaeoastronomy,* edited by A. F. Aveni, 416–429. Cambridge: Cambridge University Press.

———. (1992). *Yaxchilan: The Design of a Maya Ceremonial City.* Austin: University of Texas Press.

Thompson, J. Eric S. (1970). *Maya History and Religion.* Norman: University of Oklahoma Press.

———. (1977). "A Proposal for Constituting a Maya Subgroup, Cultural and Linguistic, in the Petén and Adjacent Regions." In *Anthropology and History in Yucatán,* edited by Grant D. Jones, 3–42. Austin: University of Texas Press.

Tozzer, Alfred M. (1903). "Report of the Fellow in American Archaeology." *American Journal of Archaeology,* 2nd series, Archaeological Institute of America, 45–49.

———. (1903). Letter of March 1. Tozzer Library, Peabody Museum, Harvard University.

———. (1907). "Survivals of Ancient Forms of Culture among the Mayas of Yucatan and the Lacandones of Chiapas." *Proceedings, Congrés International des Américanistes,* XV, Quebec 1906, Tome II: 283–288.

———. (1978 [1907]). *A Comparative Study of the Mayas and the Lacandones.* New York: AMS Press.

———. (1984 [1912]). A Spanish Manuscript Letter on the Lacandones in the Archives of the Indies at Seville. Culver City: Labyrinthos.

Wasserstrom, Robert. (1983). *Class and Society in Central Chiapas.* Berkeley: University of California Press.

Weyer, Edward. (1957). "To the Land of the Lacandones: An Expedition to a Tropical Land Where Survivors from Mayan Times Live a Secluded Existence." *Natural History* (May): 253–336.

Wilbert, Johannes. (1987). *Tobacco and Shamanism in South America.* New Haven: Yale University Press.

Ximenez, Francisco. (1929–1931). "Historia de la Provincia de San Vicente de Chiapas y Guatemala de la Orden de Predicadores." *Biblioteca Goathemala,* Vols. I–III. Guatemala: Sociedad de Geografía e Historia de Guatemala.